To my parents,
who taught me the greatest
gift I could give the world
is to be myself.

In the space between breaths I can feel it. The acceptance. The recognition. The realization that I am already whole as I am. That every glorious scar, every flaw, and insecurity only add to my completeness. And like a sharp exhale, I release my worry, the ever-present ache in my chest—I am here, I am here, I am here—and that is enough.

—NICOLE ADAIR

A LETTER TO THE READER

Dear Reader,

If you've found this book, I hope you discover a friend in the following pages. It never occurred to me to write anything other than the truth about my life and be as transparent as possible. I don't know how to live any other way, and I've never been good at hiding my emotions or ignoring them. Rather, I'm someone who wears her heart on her sleeve. I've openly expressed myself since I was a child, and though I used to believe this was one of my weaknesses, I now know it's my greatest strength.

Thus, the title of my blog and this book, *Struck Inside Out*. I believe I was not only born sensitive, but am fated to express all that I experience within—without. It's only through honoring and sharing our truths that we set ourselves free and consequently release others from their internal burdens.

I wanted my readers to have something to carry with them—something small that they could easily travel with and return to, time and time again, when needing reminders of their strength and beauty.

This book, like a loyal friend, delights in the ups and downs of our shared human experience: joyful highs like a budding new romance, inspirational pep talks before navigating uncharted paths, sprouts of wisdom learned only through discomfort, and spiritual awakenings blossomed from solitude.

The poetry and prose in this book are the life experiences that have shaped who I am today. They are not structured in chronological order as they are from various points in my life throughout the last ten years. Some of the most popular posts from my blog are scattered throughout each chapter to contribute to that chapter's theme.

In Chapters Six and Seven I've included letters to my past selves and partners. I wrote these letters with my present recollection of experiences over time. I changed the names of friends and past partners, compressed certain events, and recreated some dialogue and experiences.

The table of contents is organized by category, so if you find yourself yearning for a sad love poem, seeking encouragement to move forward with change, or desire a positive perspective on your current circumstances, you can flip to the pages that will give you what you need.

I've also included calls to action in each chapter to help you think about your life differently and make changes where you need to. There are journal prompts, fill-in-the-blank mantras, reflections, and recorded meditations for you to create a self-care practice. I encourage you to get a journal and dedicate it to the practices in this book.

Write what you're feeling. Write what you're experiencing. Write what you're observing. Finally, and most importantly, write from your heart.

We're always searching for the highest versions of ourselves. Let's embrace the journey and not just the outcome, for it's not about who we wish to be or where we hope to land, but who we become in our pursuit of something *more*.

Sending love always,
DANIELLE

WHAT I NEED TODAY
TABLE OF CONTENTS

Chapter 5: Out of the Darkness, Into the Light 101

CHAPTER 1
MORNING
INSPIRATION

Dear Reader,

Mornings are my favorite time of day. Mornings are where I meet magic. Mornings are where I inch closer to my dreams. Mornings are, quite simply, the space where I become my most authentic self.

I didn't always have this love affair with dawn and sunrises. As a teenager, my eyes only opened from sleep after 12 p.m. if it wasn't a school day. Even in my twenties, I favored the crescent moon and late-night rendezvous over rising before the rest of the world.

Now, in my thirties, I've discovered that I can do things that elevate my energy and make me feel alive in the quiet, early morning light. I can take time before my workday begins to get clear on how I want to show up for myself and others. If I practice positive habits every day, those practices become the foundation of my weeks, months, years, and ultimately, my life.

I hope you find inspiration to cultivate your own morning rituals and uncover what makes you feel great before another day begins. When you open yourself to the unlimited possibilities that each day presents, you attract new and exciting opportunities that you might not have seen before.

All it takes is getting started! Set your alarm for an hour earlier than you usually do and spend that time doing things that bring you joy. It's that simple! Once you begin this practice, you can adjust your schedule accordingly as you feel called. One hour may turn into an extra two to three hours when you start reaping the benefits of taking time for yourself. Trust yourself and your instincts upon waking, and remember to choose emotions, thoughts, and practices that serve your highest good.

That's how we change. That's how we grow. That's how we create beautiful days.

That's how powerful our mornings can become.

Sending love always,
DANIELLE

THIS IS HOW TO START YOUR DAY

When I was a teenager, I remember waking up for school only after my mom's fifth attempt at getting me to open my eyes. I'd rise from bed like a mummy from a tomb, moving toward my bedroom door in zombie-style strides. At that point, my sister had already claimed our shared bathroom space; her makeup and straightening iron would be sprawled on the vanity, and if I dared to knock on the door, screams would vibrate through the walls of our house.

I'd resort back to my room defeated, knowing that I wouldn't have enough time to wash my face, brush my teeth, do my hair and makeup, and choose an outfit I liked that wasn't my sister's clothing, as she had our dad put a padlock on her door. I had to pretend I didn't know the four-digit password while she was still upstairs, but on days when she saved enough time for breakfast, I'd crack the code and sneak into her room the moment she went downstairs. Within seconds I'd grab the first shirt or dress I saw and pray like hell we wouldn't pass each other in the hallways between classes.

Ah, the good old days.

My morning routine wasn't much of a routine when I was a teenager, and until my early twenties. My niche was a routine that consisted of zero planning or preparation and required waiting until the very last minute to do anything. I was an expert at going with the flow, rolling with the punches, and crossing my fingers that everything would just fall into place.

Now, over a decade later, mornings are the most pivotal time of my day. Mornings are where I create, plan, and focus. Mornings are the untouched page. It's the space for dreaming and getting intentional about the type of day I want to experience and the kind of life I want to lead.

Mornings are the most important time of day because you're setting the tone for how you'll feel, what you'll think, and how you'll live your life.

Here's how I use the hours just after sunrise before my workday begins:

1. MEDITATION

Most mornings, I begin my day with meditation. Some mornings I meditate for five minutes, others ten to twenty minutes. If I feel drawn to guided meditations, I'll use the Insight Timer app and search keywords like *happiness, gratitude, creativity,* or *focus.* Other times I prefer silence or the sounds of nature and set a timer for however long I want my practice to be.

I focus on my breath. When I inhale, I internally say, *I am love,* and when I exhale, *I am light.* As I repeat these mantras, I embody the energy behind those words. Sometimes I'll change the mantras depending on how I feel that day, but the main objective is to cultivate my desired energy. Feeling the positivity behind my thoughts is just as important, if not more, than only thinking happy thoughts.

2. JOURNALING, AFFIRMATIONS, AND MANIFESTATION

I have a journal filled with positive affirmations, gratitude lists, and detailed narratives of the life I want to live. When I read this journal, I instantly feel love and excitement for my life, as I've filled the pages with everything that makes me inspired.

After I meditate, I'll open the journal and write:

- Any thoughts, ideas, or visions that came to me during my meditation.
- Five to ten things that I'm grateful for. These can be things that happened the day prior, gifts in the present moment, or general things I feel lucky to have. I always explain *why* I'm grateful for them.
- My dreams as though they already happened, giving rich details of what I'm excited to have and experience. For example, "I'm so grateful that I'm a successful business owner and help people lead fulfilling lives!"
- Positive affirmations on the type of person I want to be and the kind of life I want to live. For example, "I'm the most positive person I know." "I cultivate magic in my everyday life." "I only attract loving people and experiences."

If you have an oracle card deck that you use, I'd suggest pulling a card or a few cards after your meditation and asking for messages that will help you throughout the day. When I ask for a message to support and guide me, I always get an answer.

3. EXERCISING

Moving your body for at least thirty minutes a day helps increase blood flow and boost endorphins to aid happiness and optimal health. I typically try to do this in the morning before my mind brainstorms excuses not to do it later in the day. It also makes me feel invigorated, and I'd prefer to start my day with that energy.

I like to go for a three-mile run and then follow up with a fifteen-to-thirty-minute workout.

You might find the same satisfaction in a long walk, yoga, Pilates, weightlifting, or kickboxing. Whatever your preference is, carve out at least thirty minutes to move your body for a natural high.

4. REFOCUSING YOUR ATTENTION ON WHERE YOU WANT IT TO BE

When I'm getting ready for work, I sometimes find myself ten steps ahead of where I am. Although my body may be in front of a mirror, my brain is already sitting at my office desk juggling ten things at once. I can get so anxious and stressed when thinking about to-do lists that I forget I have the power to think about my workday differently. Yes, there may be a lot to get done, but instead of worrying about not completing everything, I can choose to focus on one thing at a time and know that everything will eventually be crossed off my list.

I also don't want to get into the habit of rushing my day or life by living everywhere else except in the present moment. So, I bring my awareness back into the present by focusing on my breath, observing my surroundings, and *choosing* what I'll center my energy on.

5. INTENTIONAL DANCING

Lastly, some mornings when I feel like I can't shake grogginess, negativity, or monotony no matter what I do, I put on a favorite song and dance around my living room. I move my body. I don't care how I look. I let myself breathe, dance, and just be silly.

Moving this way increases my energy levels and reminds me that life can be funny and goofy. Even if I don't feel like doing something, I am not my initial thoughts or feelings. I am what I *choose* to think and feel. Playing a good song and letting myself dance for the sake of dancing shakes me out of a mundane mindset and offers the space to be and enjoy being.

These are just a few tips for beginning your day with gratitude, movement, and happiness. What works for me might not work for you but give some of these activities a try and then modify your morning routine to what naturally feels good.

Remember, this human experience is up to you. You get to choose what thoughts you're thinking, what emotions you're feeling, and what space you'll inhabit. It can be as easy or as difficult as you make it. The more conscious you are of your thoughts and habits, the more you'll create a life that fulfills and sustains you, uplifts and excites you, and jolts you out of bed in the morning without having to hit snooze.

Who hits snooze on a life they're excited about anyway?

LOOK FOR THE BIRDS

I look out the window and see a family of birds rummaging for
breakfast on a blanket of dewy grass.

There's a robin with her mate, flying in circles midair,
gracefully embracing their lover's dance.

A cardinal lands on the arm of a tree, unconcerned with
his surroundings, content with himself and the rays of light warming his
wings.

Three doves peck and scavenge through soil. One keeps her
distance from the other two. Perhaps she has lost her eternal spouse.

Flying high in the sky, a chorus of geese soar in unison, each aware of
their next synchronized movement, for this early morning voyage is a
passage of unity.

There's something miraculous about sitting in solitude on a warm spring morning in nature. I like to observe my surroundings upon waking as I sit at my desk, which faces two large open windows. I let the breeze roll in and graze my skin; I feel gratitude for the sun's warmth resting on my hands as they type; and I breathe in the power of a new season—a season that births growth, new beginnings, and positive change.

During these mornings of quiet and peace, I'm reminded to open my eyes and look around me. What sounds are being brought to my ears? What sights are set before me? What emotions are taking place within me? What scents are drifting in from the window? How can I simply be here in this moment without being distracted by anything but my senses?

Most days, I get caught up in the busyness of life and unhealthy addictions to technology. But lately, if I'm sitting in my office, driving in my car, walking to a coffee shop, or stepping outside for fresh air, I've noticed that I often look to the sky and watch the birds. I become entranced by their swaying and gliding through the air. The way they careen above and below the wind's current.

They've become a reminder to step back into the present moment. They remind me that there's always life outside of my perspective. Other worlds exist around me all the time. Animals fly, insects crawl, squirrels jump from tree to tree, spiders spin webs, and caterpillars patiently await their evolution into butterflies.

How often do I notice this?

Have you taken time today to breathe, look at your world, and appreciate your view? Have you listened to the choir of birds in the nearest tree? Can you understand that everything you see, feel, taste, and touch is meant for you?

You are alive.

You are here.

You are meant to experience all of this.

This marvelous and beautiful world.

Are you listening?

Are you watching?

Are you letting it in?

This life is for you, dear one.

Don't forget to look around or you may miss it.

STEP OUTSIDE

Wherever you are right now, can you pause for a moment and step outside? Using your five senses, experience the natural world around you. Be present with this moment and everything it offers.

What can you experience with awakened senses? How

does the current moment feel when you give your entire self to it? How does your perception change when you live in the present moment with a conscious gaze?

START DOING THIS NOW

I get excited to write about elevating the ordinary because everyone can do this, but most people aren't aware of their ability to do so. Our mindset is our power. How we choose to see ourselves, others, and our everyday existence says a lot about who we are.

When we change how we look at the elements of our lives, the elements of our lives change.

Oftentimes, though, we become too familiar with thinking the same thoughts, repeating rote scripts, and performing habituated ways of being that we lose sight of the very thing we try to avoid as much as possible—a routine and humdrum life.

Time feels like it's flying because we allow ourselves to slip into an autopilot lifestyle where we repeatedly respond to experiences in the same way.

If you really want to refresh your life, notice your hourly thoughts. Observe your triggers, how you talk to people, the phrases and comments you speak daily, how you feel when you arrive at work or return home, and how you manage your free time. There's a lot to be said for the space you choose to live your life from.

Are you someone who's always rushed?

Do you have patience for those around you?

Are you constantly getting annoyed at the same things?

Do you talk to yourself the way you talk to others?

Do you talk to others the way you talk to yourself?

Do you let other people's actions or words affect your mood?

Are you always judging yourself or those around you?

Do you get tired of hearing yourself think and speak what you're thinking and speaking?

Are you always struggling to get through the day or week until you're free from responsibility?

The path to living a passionate, purposeful, and meaningful life is woven throughout our small daily actions.

We all want the best possible lives for ourselves. Most times, when we imagine our ideal existence, we look toward a fictional future where our problems cease to exist, and everything is exactly as we desire. We see wealth, freedom, love, happiness, and adventure. We believe that with hard work and determination, we will one day reach that place of unadulterated bliss.

The truth, though? You can achieve a certain level of bliss (even unadulterated bliss) if you stop placing your happiness months or years ahead of you and focus on what makes your life fascinating now.

To discover fascination in what you deem ordinary, do the opposite of your instincts.

Are you constantly arguing with your partner? Experiment with a different mindset. Learn to let things go. Communicate more clearly. Think of all the reasons why you fell in love with this person. Take more time for yourself.

Do you get aggravated with coworkers or your boss? Instead of focusing on everything you dislike within someone, challenge yourself for a week or more to seek out his or her redeeming qualities. Even if you find it difficult to do so, you'll become a kinder and less judgmental person in the process.

Do you speed on your commute and get frustrated with other drivers? (This is me!) Don't look at your phone while driving. Instead, put on a song or podcast that you don't usually listen to. Let other drivers get in front of you. Observe new things you've never noticed on your daily commute.

Do you struggle with waking up in the morning? Commit to making more time for yourself as much as you make time for everything and everyone else. Promise yourself that you'll no longer put yourself and your well-being second to anything or anyone.

Are you tired of coming home exhausted at the end of the day and watching TV or going on your phone or computer for hours? Toward the end of your day, drink a full glass of water and say the mantra to yourself or aloud, *I am alive. I am awake. I am present. I am well.* Say it and feel it. Do something different that you haven't done in a while, or ever. Read a book. Call a friend. Go for a walk. Gaze at the stars. Write in a journal. Go on a coffee date. Be by yourself. Be with someone else. Whatever it is, try something new.

I challenge you to notice how you go about your days and rewire your brain to react to negative triggers the opposite way to how you usually would.

When a friend, partner, or coworker says something triggering, reach for a higher thought and respond with positivity. If you're at work and anxiety settles in, remember that you can choose how you'll feel throughout your day. When you're rushing home to eat dinner in front of the TV, remember that this moment is your life. Why are you rushing it? Why are you wishing it away?

What space will you choose to live from?

How will you make your ordinary world something extraordinary?

When will you begin choosing happiness now?

The choice is always yours.

PROMISE ME ONE THING

Promise me one thing.

Promise me that you'll take today moment by moment. Notice the sounds and smells that lighten you and the tastes and sights that lift you. Look for your joy and dwell alongside it in recognition. Remember, this life is not meant to be rushed. We aren't in a race. We can always embrace stillness.

I hope you don't spend your hours looking toward the clock, waiting for the moment that you're free from responsibility. I know the hours can feel long, the pressure too hard to handle, but if we speed through this moment, we're hastening our one precious life. What if today was all we had?

Please promise me that you'll meet yourself in the quiet. The present. Where all creation exists. Please tell me that you'll look for your bliss as much as you seek your pain. Promise me that you won't take this day for granted. That it won't become another checked box on your calendar so that tomorrow comes sooner.

Today is all we have. This moment is a gift. Remember to explore your blessings and reach for the gold-threaded throughout the day. You'll have your highs and your lows, and that's okay. We're meant to exist between both worlds. Breathe through the moments when you fall and savor in the miracles when you rise. Both offer gifts. Both are beautiful.

Just as you are.

Just as today is.
Just as this moment can become.

MOMENTS TO SAVOR

What are three to five things you're looking forward to experiencing today? These can be simple: your chai latte, meeting a friend for lunch, trying a new recipe for dinner, or watching a new episode of your favorite show. Write down the little things that will bring you joy today and explain why you're grateful for them.

Life holds gifts we can open every single day; we just need to open our eyes to see them.

FINDING DIVINITY IN THE ORDINARY

I lay in bed staring at the white ceiling, feeling the sun glare through the blinds. I take three deep breaths before I plant my feet on the ground. I let gratitude slide down my spine and baptize my body with a freshened awareness for the new day.

I begin the usual routine of splashing water on my face, brushing my teeth, making a cup of coffee, opening the windows to let fresh air in, and getting ready for work. Today feels the same as yesterday. I'm going about the traditional order of things yet trying to find divinity in the ordinary.

Finding divinity in the ordinary and seeking sanctity in the familiar separates a banal life from an exceptional one. If we live solely growing off the graces of the pleasurable moments, the freedom from Friday to Sunday, or in our future escapes, then we're missing the treasures that exist between those spaces.

We're warriors during the week. We battle constant distractions, rise when we want to remain still, and encompass the highs and lows of being human. There's honor, virtue, and growth in that.

This is the essential in-between space that we often don't value in our pursuit of liberation.

What would we be without it, though? Where would any stretching or movement occur without the occasional morning angst, the fear of continuing forward, and the desire to simply stay put?

These are our triggers. These are the buttons we push that bring us to a heightened awareness of ourselves. Without them, we wouldn't expand.

We need the in-between. We need the rough spaces. We need them not only to bring us back into the light but to remind us of the duality of our beings.

The beauty of our beings.

The potential to be more at peace than we ever conceived.

GRACE IN THE ROUGH SPACES

What triggers and low points greet you most weekdays? Where do you fall rather than rise? What buttons get pushed day after day?

Is there a glimpse of grace in your daily or weekly battles? Can you see the piles of laundry, the dishes in the sink, the endless errands, or your lack of sleep as an essential part of the balancing act of being human? Is it possible that our ordinary annoyances emphasize our ease and pleasure? Can the two coexist in harmony rather than contempt?

You Are the Life
You Choose to Live

Today I find thanks in the natural flow of my life. I know that my heart longs for an existence beyond my wildest dreams, but there's immense beauty in the delicate moments of my days. I will search for it. I will find it. I will hold it close.

Today I offer sincere gratitude for my many jobs and responsibilities. I know I can feel overwhelmed. I know that I worry I'm not doing enough. I know that I fear I'll never get to where I want to be. But today, I'm learning to love the messy, the busy, the never-ceasing journey toward fulfilling my dreams.

Today I give thanks for the quiet night. I honor the time when I'm alone to think, reflect, create, and bask in solitude. I thank this moment of my life where I'm my own best friend. I'm deeply thankful for my own company.

Today I'm grateful for the triggers, the people who test me, the experiences that hurt me, and the obstacles I currently face. They are teaching me strength, insight, and the grace of great change.

Today I find thanks for the mere act of offering gratitude. I can believe that my life will get better in the future, or I can make my life better now.

Ease into your cycles. Bless your sacred journey. Love the rhythm of yourself in motion.

Your outlook is the key to your freedom.

The gaze you hold is your power.

You are the life you choose to live.

Journal Prompts for Inspired Living

- What's one habit you can let go of that isn't serving your highest good?
- What's one habit you can incorporate into your schedule to help you be happier, more fulfilled, and productive?
- What are the top five things in your life right now that you're grateful to have? Why?
- What are the top five things that you want to work toward achieving and becoming? Why?
- What small step can you take today to move you closer to your dreams?
- How can you stay motivated to continue with practices that serve you rather than weigh you down?
- What daily reminders can you tell yourself to inspire you to continue forward?
- What's one positive affirmation that you can write down on a piece of paper and tape to your bathroom mirror?
- What's your favorite activity to do outside and why? Can you make time for it at least three times a week? Make a plan for how you'll do this.
- Write about a day in the life of your dreams. Write in the present tense and add as much detail as you can. For example, what do you start your day doing? What do you eat for breakfast? What does your home look like? Where are you located? What do you wear? What restaurants do you go to for lunch?

Where do you shop? How do you feel? Who are you with? How do you make others feel? What is your primary purpose and passion?

- Have fun with this! The more specific you are, the more real your goals will feel and the more motivation you'll have to go after your dreams.

Chapter 2
Meditative
Awakenings

Dear Reader,

I'm a lover of meditation in all its forms. Most people believe that in order to meditate, you must be sitting cross-legged with your thumb and middle finger connected, eyes closed, and in a zen state. Truthfully, you can reap the benefits of meditation through other outlets outside of complete silence and stillness.

Writing, for me, is meditation. Going for walks and runs through wooded trails is meditation. Laying in an open field watching the sunset is meditation. Closing my eyes and focusing on my breath is meditation.

Meditation is what helps transport you into the present moment. It guides you to your truth. It enables you to see what your eyes can't decipher but what your soul understands as home.

When you tune into this space as often as you can, you'll awaken dormant bursts of wisdom that help you lead your life. All the answers you need are inside of you.

This chapter includes some awakenings I've experienced from entering a meditative state. At the end of this chapter, you'll find a meditation that you can do on your own to inspire you to uncover the paradise that exists within you. This meditation teaches you to tap into your intuition and provides questions about living a more purposeful life. You can use these questions as journal prompts to dive into your soul's truth.

I hope you discover many awakenings—now and always.

Sending love always,
DANIELLE

THERE IS GOLD
WITHIN

There was a time when I believed that this life was what it was, that I had no control over the ebbs and flows, the constant vacillation between happy and sad, and the fiery hunger to be more than I was.

There was a time when I thought I would eternally float through life asleep. I thought I was the girl staring at me in the mirror, the person others perceived me to be, the longing in my writing, the static energy that came when I couldn't sleep.

I didn't know that I needed to sit. I needed to be still. I needed a breath of air so big and expansive that it could fill the entirety of my being. I needed a breath to remind me that I could breathe.

There was a time when I would turn to others to answer all my questions. To tell me how to feel and what to say. I didn't trust myself. I didn't believe I could answer my own soul.

I didn't know that I was the source, the knower, the limitless sky, the glistening light, my own home.

I wish someone would have told me when I was lost in the darkness looking for validation that the only place I needed to look was within.

There is an astounding presence within me that whispers, *I am enough. I am love. I have everything I need inside of me. Keep going. I am doing so well. Continue returning to love.*

I try to remember these words when I awake to an anxious pit in my stomach, not knowing why I feel unready for the day. I return to this voice when I fall asleep to a clamoring of thoughts hastening through my brain. I call on this higher self when I need encouragement to believe in my dreams.

I am my highest self when I meet myself in the silent abyss, in the rising and falling of my chest, in the visions and sounds that reveal themselves to me when my eyes are closed.

I begin this day knowing that I am already whole. I need nothing outside of myself, for there is gold within. I am the seeker, the knower, the giver, the receiver, the endless expanse of creation manifest.

You are enough. You are love. You have everything you need inside of you. Keep going. You are doing so well. Continue returning to love.

A RENEWED SELF

There's something inside of me waiting to be seen. I feel it seated within me, softly lingering until I become still and recognize its divinity.

It's been drifting at the base of my stomach my whole life, even before birth. It comes and goes, gracefully revealing itself to me when I allow myself to unravel. When I take the time not to think, speak, go anywhere or do anything, but rather sit and breathe.

In and out.

In and out.

How do I get lost and forget about you? How can I travel miles away and not see that you're always part of me?

Sometimes it takes distance and being led astray to find my way back to you. All I must do is close my eyes, take a deep breath, and exhale long and slow to see that you have risen from the depths of my stomach and into the corners of my heart. It's from this space that I see things clearly. I understand myself and why I'm here. I feel immense gratitude shine over me like pure sunlight. My anxieties, worries, and fears fall into the fire, burning, with their embers rising into the sky.

Now that I've found you again, I ask you not to leave. When I choose busyness, late nights, delayed mornings, gossip, and chatter, please remember me. Reveal yourself through a stranger's voice, the illumination of constellations, the tender hush of autumn, and the emblems in my dreams.

I know what I'm meant for. To become who I am, part of me must die.

Am I willing to let her go? Will I be okay when I lose the identities I've created? Will there still be people by my side?

I don't know the woman waiting at the end of the dandelion field waving at me, but I'm stepping forward into a renewed sense of self.

I'm asking for an awakened awareness to lead me home.

GIFTS FROM THE DARK

Do you ever feel like pushing out the darkness? Do you ever conceive of escaping the eclipse? Whenever the wave of discomfort rolls over you like cold water at the break of dawn, do you pull the covers back over your face to hide from the hurt, to avoid the unease?

When I was younger, I would brace myself for heartache and loneliness by assuming the worst of my pain and trying to run from it.

I felt ashamed for abandoning my joy, for not always feeling bliss. I didn't want to confront the blank space, the heavy heart, the thoughts that kept me from sleep. Instead, I would close my eyes and hope that with the sunrise I would wake anew, reborn, replenished, and cleansed of all aches.

As the months passed, I learned to greet the guest staying with me. I understood that she, like joy, brought gifts with her. But, to receive these gifts, I had to sit and converse with her. I had to draw a roadmap of where she was coming from, why she was here, and where she was going after leaving me.

After years of fearing the eclipse, I now know that it's merely the shadowing of the sun, never the removal of its light. Its beams are eternally present no matter what our landscapes appear to be.

Every person that enters your scenery, any memory that weighs on your heart, each pang of sadness that etches across your chest is a gift. Even these dimmed spaces of our souls have a beauty far beyond what our eyes can see.

We must embrace the totality of our beings to receive these graces.

I now welcome the unknown. I see every new circumstance that greets me as the teacher I once asked for. I find meaning in the annoyances, the sometimes-rote routine, empty conversations with others, and the worries my mind can drift into believing. I listen as though they are secrets from the divine.

For when the light is darkened by shadows, the sun forever remains.

REMEMBERING MY SOUL MEDITATION

Listen to this meditation on Struck Inside Out's *website. See "Additional Resources" at the end of the book for the link to access it.*

I remember being a little girl and sitting on the floor of my room, staring at myself in the mirror. I'd observe the pores stretched across my cheeks, the tiny hairs perked up on my eyelids, and the button shape of my nose as though I were seeing myself for the first time. I'd run my fingers along my face, feeling the smoothness of my skin. I'd stare at the reflection of my eyes for so long that my face would eventually become blurred. Then I'd blink and refocus my eyes for clarity again.

I remember feeling like a foreigner in my body.

As a young girl, I was aware of the temporality of this life and that my body was merely a vehicle for my soul. When I engaged in a staring match with my reflection, I knew I was only seeing one version of myself. This physical adaptation represented only a tiny fraction of who I was.

The truth of my being was that I was all-knowing, all-powerful, and already whole, even when I didn't usually feel that way. The truth of my soul was that I came here to learn lessons, create relationships, and experience the magnificent mystery of being alive in human form.

I've always known this, but as is the nature of life, I slipped in and out of remembering.

As I got older and welcomed the sweetness of first love, the anguish of loss, and the understanding that my existence felt astonishing and daunting, I learned to trust the instincts growing within me. They were showing me how to live. They were teaching me how to love.

Some days I absorbed guidance like rain seeping into soil; others, I didn't know how to rely on the emotions speaking to me.

This dance with intuition and the nature of my soul is an ongoing ballad that lifts me from ordinary life and into union with the divine. The more I listen, respect, and trust, the deeper my well of knowledge grows.

The more connected to myself I become.

The more I'm my own confidant, advisor, and friend.

You, too, have this bond with your soul. The soul that's lived many lifetimes and has traveled through the vastness of the universe. The soul that already knows everything it needs to.

If you feel disconnected from your voice, close your eyes, be still, and ask that it speak to you. Ask that you hear, see, and feel the messages meant for you. Ask that it be easy. Ask that it feels like returning home.

Focus on your breath. Allow the inhale to arrive in your body like the tide meets the shore. Then, release it as though the ripples are returning to the waves.

Feel your breath coming in through your nose and then release it through your mouth. Breathe long and slowly. Exhale long and slowly.

What do you want to work on? What are you seeking answers to? How do you want to feel?

Mentally ask yourself a question. You're going to allow the answers to come to you.

Maybe you want clarity on your life's purpose or the meaning of a relationship. Maybe you want to know your next steps regarding a specific situation. Or maybe you're looking for a general message for the day.

Don't worry that the answers won't arrive, and don't

force an answer to appear. Instead, simply sit in silence and observe yourself.

What sensations are you feeling?

What visions are you seeing?

What scents are you smelling?

What sounds are you hearing?

Whatever it is that arises, don't judge it. Don't try to label it. Don't force it to be anything other than what it is.

Simply allow the answers to enter your awareness and treat them as though they're unexpected teachers. Let them speak to you in their unique way.

Now, ask once more if there's anything else you need to know. Continue to observe and listen.

Thank yourself for taking the time to tap into your intuition. Honor the wisdom that resides within you. Bless yourself for speaking to your higher self.

Take one deeper inhale and lift your hands above your head. Then, exhale and drop them to your heart in prayer position.

Say the following to yourself or aloud: *The answers I need are within me. I deepen my connection to my intuition and my source of wisdom every day. I trust myself to guide me through life. I am my own best friend and confidant. I always know the way.*

Thank you.

And whenever you're ready, bring some movement back into your fingers and toes, and open your eyes.

Reflect and Record
Your Insights

Now that you've experimented with using your senses to understand your intuition, grab your journal and write about the experience.

How did you feel throughout the meditation?

What visions presented themselves to you?

What sounds did you hear?

What scents did you smell?

What sensations did you experience?

What was your biggest takeaway?

How do you feel now that the meditation is over?

Even if you didn't experience many sensations, that's okay and perfectly normal. The more you practice meditation and utilize your intuition, the stronger it becomes. Like working a muscle at the gym, your intuition grows more powerful as you practice using it.

Everything that presents itself to you during your practice is a sign. If you're having trouble focusing and can't keep your thoughts in one place, that is a message. It could represent you feeling distracted in your life. Outside noises preventing you from completely tuning into the meditation could signify a noisy lifestyle where you're being asked to make room for rest and quiet. If you saw animals, nature, people, words, or phrases, think of what those images specifically mean to you. The same goes for any scent, sound, or sensation you experienced.

Write anything else you'd like to share and remember: the more you return to this space, the easier accessing your intuition becomes, and the more you'll trust yourself to guide you through life.

CHAPTER 3
ENCOURAGING
MANTRAS

Dear Reader,

One thing I'm passionate about is making the everyday existence of life something magical (if you haven't already noticed).

If we spend three-quarters of our lives working and living in a "mundane," wishful space, we must ask ourselves: how can we transform the humdrum way of life into something meaningful? Is it possible to take a random weekday and infuse it with the type of energy we bring into the weekend?

Our magic exists in our perspective. We feel unenthused by life because we've chosen to view our world through a dull lens. Instead of dreading your workdays, commute, or interactions with coworkers, think about a simple shift in perspective that can make the familiar intriguing. Where have you lost sight of your blessings? How often do you focus on lack rather than abundance? In what ways can you begin implementing positive thoughts and practices to support the life you're living *now*?

Before real change occurs, we must become grateful for all we have. When you make what you have become *enough* for you, you welcome new forms of prosperity.

This chapter is filled with reflections on everyday life and mantras to help you think about your life in more positive and meaningful ways. At the end of this chapter, you can create your own mantras to help make the familiar something exquisite and rare.

Sending love always,
DANIELLE

A MANTRA FOR
MONDAYS

Today I need to...
Breathe. I need to remember that Monday is merely a name that humans manufactured to help organize their days. To believe in her reputation of being a burden is to rob myself of the loveliness of another new day. Names are simply labels we create to assist in our understanding of things. If I change the way I look at things, the things I look at change.

Today I want to...
Do something out of the ordinary. How many Mondays before this have I lived in the same old patterns? I can give in to the tiredness and lack of motivation or choose a new path and believe that today is one of my favorite days. Mondays are where it all begins for me. Today I choose to experience my moments with a sense of wonder. The possibilities are endless when I open my mind to new outcomes.

Today I will...
Be the bearer of light for those I meet. I know everyone is carrying their own struggles that I know nothing about. All it takes is a smile, a kind gesture, genuine listening, an honest reply to someone's question, and the willingness to experiment with new ways of being for this day to become one of new beginnings. Today is the start of another weekly adventure where I can lift others while raising my own vibration.

Today I promise to...

Live with purpose. I will remember that each day offers the opportunity to grow, love, and enjoy being alive. I will not rush another day of my life because I'm waiting for the weekend, my next vacation, or the moment for me to be truly happy. The moment I'm living right now deserves the appreciation that all my future ones do. I am grateful for this moment; this moment is my life.

Today I am...

Changing my perception of what I usually believe. It's easy to fall into societal patterns and turn on auto-pilot when coming off the high of a weekend, but it will benefit me and those around me if I choose to be awake. I look around at my everyday surroundings—my home, car, job, weekly plans, relationships—and I see how lucky I am to have everything *exactly* as it is. I wouldn't change a thing in this perfect moment, on this perfect Monday, of another new week.

When I can find the beauty in the ordinary, I welcome and accept the extraordinary.

On Mondays, I take my first step on a new exploration of life.

Today is the day when all good things are born.

All is well in my world.

THE POWER OF MONDAYS

We give a lot of credit to January 1st, the day we begin our New Year's resolutions. We view the first day of January as the start of a better life where we can mold our resolutions into a sparkling new lifestyle we weren't able to create the year before.

But what about the start of a new week? Why does the first month of the year only have transformational powers? Why can't Monday possess the same potential?

It's interesting that the day people typically dread the most is the day we can put our resolutions into practice to create the changes we say we desire every year. Monday is perfect for setting intentions, implementing positive habits, and reminding yourself why you show up for your life in the way you do. If you begin the week on a strong note, you'll carry that energy throughout the rest of your week.

What's one productive habit you can practice on Mondays to create excitement for a new week?

How can you change the narrative from having the "Monday blues" to being grateful for another day of life?

Where can you enhance your typical thought patterns to focus on the possibilities Mondays offer, rather than everything it takes away?

EMBRACING COMPLETE ACCEPTANCE

I felt the energy of complete acceptance for all that is this morning.

I wasn't rushing, controlling, or forcing anything to be different. I simply trusted where I was. I loved who I was. I embraced the path I was on. I welcomed this beautiful new moment I was reveling in.

Most days, I feel this urgency to create and produce—to push myself further into my desires. But this morning, I didn't need to propel myself into a future I know I'll inevitably meet.

I simply sat with the blessings of everything I've created thus far. I trusted that whatever I'm meant to do and whoever I'm destined to be with won't miss me. It will find me just as I inch closer toward it.

How beautiful is that realization? To not always race toward where you believe you're supposed to be, but instead, embody everything you are. Doesn't that feel more secure than the perpetual chase of a different life?

There is divinity in who you are now, precisely because of who you are.

There is grace in where you are now, precisely because of where you are.

There are blessings in everything, precisely because of all that is.

Love who and where you are now without always looking toward the horizon.

You are beautiful.

You are perfect.
You are exactly where you're meant to be.

Pursue Beauty in the Blank Spaces

Most mornings, I sit at my desk to write. I look out the window and take in the blue sky. I feel a warm breeze graze my cheeks. I listen to families of birds combing the grass for early morning treats. And I hope that with the scent of summer's heat, inspiration will come soaring through the open window.

Most days, I seem to focus on the lack of trees in mine and the neighbors' yards. I'm a tree lover. I love big, old, canopying trees that house different types of animals and offer fresh shade on hot afternoons. I love laying on blankets underneath a mantle of branches blooming with green. I love nights under mighty oaks as I catch flickering starlight beneath swaying leaves. I'm a real lover of grass below bare feet and the endless majestic wonder of nature.

After Hurricane Sandy hit New York in 2012, most of the trees around my house died and were cut down. Since then, I have found myself seeing blank spaces that should be brimming with new life. In between the trees still standing, all my eyes focus on is absence.

This is a fitting metaphor for my life sometimes.

How many days have I looked out the window to see a lack of something? How long have I ignored the beauty already standing before me, begging to be seen?

There are numerous days when I tell myself that I will appreciate the little things. I affirm that I'll start cultivating gratitude in the simple moments of life so I can shift my perception to positivity.

I say...

I will choose to be happy at my job that offers sustenance for monthly bills, road trips, nights out with friends, and the everyday necessities of life.

I will be grateful for my bills because they represent energy circulation. Money is a form of energy, and bills remind me that I have the resources to pay for things I want and need.

I will feel the warmth of a genuine circle of friends and family who support and nourish me.

I will respect the allegiance of an ever-growing love that surprises me every day with how significant and rare I can feel.

I will honor my journey, knowing that I don't need to be where everyone else is, and everyone doesn't need to be where I am. We are all exactly where we need to be.

I will adjust my vision to see what's present rather than what's not.

I will pursue the beauty in the blank spaces.

I will look for the trees already standing.

MANTRAS FOR COPING WITH DIFFICULT TIMES

I allow myself to feel upset when I need to. My emotions are temporary. This difficult time will pass.

I can and will overcome any challenge.

Hard times teach me my power of choice. My power lies in how I choose to view hard times.

I cultivate self-compassion, patience, and understanding.

When life feels difficult, I can exercise resiliency.

It is safe for me to feel negativity or sadness because I know that I can always change my thoughts and emotions when I desire a higher vibration.

I take today moment by moment. I take this week day by day.

I am allowed to see things the way I want to see them,

even if the way I am seeing them causes me pain. I trust in myself to know what emotions are best for me in this moment.

It's okay if I don't understand myself or my life right now. I don't always need to have the answers.

I have myself, my love, and my own support. That can be enough for me right now.

To the Start of a New Day

Some days it feels easy to cultivate a positive perspective. On other days, it requires effort. Regardless of how I feel when I wake up, I try to speak lovingly to myself and the new day before me.

I say the following affirmations to myself at the start of a new day.

You can say to yourself whatever works best for you and your unique lifestyle.

To the start of a new day...

Thank you for a clean slate, a fresh start, and another chance to learn, grow, and evolve.

Thank you for the blanket that warms me, the pillow I rest my head on, the bed that holds me, the window that lets in rays of sun.

Thank you for my feet that support me as I get out of bed. My arms that reach for the ceiling as I stretch into the early morning hours. My long hair that I run my fingers through. The teeth that I brush and the face that I cleanse. I am healthy. I am whole. I am complete.

Thank you for my fridge filled with food. My coffee to help awaken me. The car that I listen to music in during my commute to work. The safety of another trip to my office.

Thank you for my desk and the office that I work in so I can support myself. Thank you for the bills I can afford and the opportunity to plan dinners, nights out, and vacations with my income.

Thank you for my coworkers, staff, boss, and the opportunity to create meaningful relationships with people while I work.

Thank you for the ability to connect with others and share my light with those around me. These relationships are in my life for a reason. I will value them.

Thank you for the occasional stress, the worrisome thought, and the fear of change. These emotions remind me to realign myself with what's true and not disregard the lower vibrations within me. Each emotion has its purpose.

Thank you for the setting of the sun, the sweet winter sky, and the moon that shines and reminds me of life's many mysteries.

Thank you for the warm apartment that I come home to, the people I love that reside in my home, and the space that reflects my inner temple.

Thank you for the ordinary and regular flow of life.

Thank you for my dreams, both in my sleep and while awake. Thank you for the possibility of more, the prospect of the new, for the endless beauty and wealth that always surround me.

Thank you for the opportunity to be myself in a world of other searching souls.

Thank you for my one cherished life.

I'm grateful for this, all that is, and all that will be.

I thank you.

THINGS I WISH I
LEARNED WHEN I WAS
YOUNGER

I wish someone would have told me from an early age that I have all I will ever need inside of me, that if I ever feel lost or unsure, I must simply look within.

I wish I had known from birth that my power lies in my intention. Through choosing my thoughts, listening to my emotions, and nurturing my soul, I create my inner and outer worlds.

I wish these truths coursed through my veins like a river flowing downstream. I want to be drenched in the cold veracity of my life, to be taken under the current so forcibly that my lungs breathe in the flood.

When I forget the nature of my being and slip into old patterns, when I invite others to take up space in my body, when I drink to the point of losing all control, I must remember to dip my feet into the glacial stream. To drink from the source that nurtures me.

I wish someone would have told me that even in my darkest hour, there's a light that flickers like a single wick in an abandoned home, and when I focus on this flare, it can fill an entire room with radiance.

How could I have known that my passage through nightfall and the winding trails that led me into the most desolate solitude would be my greatest gift? Why am I afraid of what rises when the moon does? Why do I run from my pain without coming to understand it first? How have we been conditioned to live this way?

I was born to live wholly, courageously, and without restraint. I'm meant to be free and house immense, imaginative dreams. I was not intended to wake and sleep in continual monotony. I was not made for the traditional. My soul is ravenous for the fresh and purposeful.

I'm a beacon of light. I come from the light. I live in the light. I'm always headed toward the light.

When I remember the nature of who I am, why I'm here, and what I'm meant to do, then I'm free to experience life as my heart desires.

I wish I had known that even though I learned this in my later years, it was always meant to be this way. Our wisdom is rooted like seeds within us. Until we recognize them and see their potential to bloom, they patiently sit waiting to be watered.

I wish that I would no longer wish for anything. My life is perfect as it is. I am perfect as I am.

I hope as I go to sleep tonight that I tell the story I want to hear.

I hope when I wake tomorrow, I write the story I want to live.

I hope this for you, too.

I hope you realize the truth of who you are and why you're here.

I hope you discover the bravery to follow your destined path.

I hope you harvest the courage to do whatever it takes to become yourself.

In Retrospect

There are many things we wish we had learned from an earlier age to make our present lives easier. How nice would it be if someone laid out every challenge, heartbreak, and loss we were bound to experience and told us precisely how to get through it? Wouldn't our lives have been a lot less painful if we were taught every lesson from birth?

Of course, that's not why we're here. Part of our life's purpose is to learn these lessons on our own, and we tend to learn the most from our struggles.

What's one thing you wish you had learned when you were younger and how has your life changed for the better because you learned it on your own?

How has the very thing that challenged you the most become something you wouldn't change if you had the chance to do it over again?

MANTRAS FOR A
MEANINGFUL LIFE

Create your own mantras to support the life you're living and the life you want to live. Use the prompts below to elevate your perspective on yourself and your life.

1. Form a statement that explains why you're grateful for your current source of income and why you're blessed to have your job.

2. Create mantras that encompass love for the smaller things in life that we often take for granted. For example, your morning cup of coffee, having air conditioning or heating in your home, using your five senses, enjoying someone's company, a bout of deep laughter, encouraging words from a book, the beauty of flowers, the peace of nature, etc.

3. Write a sentence that transforms your triggers into your teachers. How do the people or experiences that bother you most teach you more about yourself? Start your sentence with, "I'm lucky to have _____, because it's teaching me _____." Try to be as descriptive as possible with the lessons you're learning from your triggers.

4. Construct a statement that converts the things you dread most about your life, work, and relationships into steppingstones that lead you toward where you want to be. What are you learning from the dreaded aspects of your life that help you understand what

you *do* want, what you *can* feel, and who you *will* become?

5. Produce three mantras that include:

   a. Your love and appreciation for your physical body and all it enables you to do.
   b. Your gratitude for all your choices that led you to this moment.
   c. Your trust and faith in your future to deliver all you want to feel and achieve.

6. What are your favorite things about yourself and your life? Do you love your hair, skin, eyes, or curves? Do you appreciate your confidence, kindness, empathy, or motivation? Do you love the people in your life, the income you earn, where you live, or your possessions? Whatever you love most about yourself and your life, make a list of those things. Start each sentence with: "One of my favorite things about myself/my life is _____ because _____." Try to create as many sentences as you can and enjoy the process of doing so.

7. What are some of the hardest obstacles you've overcome? Do you remember when going through those challenges how you thought you'd never get over them? What did those challenges teach you about yourself? Write a few sentences about your strength and resilience during some of the hardest parts of your life. For example: "I have proven to myself that I am strong and can handle anything." "I love how positive and resilient I can be." "I learned from _____ that I am equipped to endure any storm."

8. Who is your ideal self? What type of person do you dream of becoming? Is it someone kind, compassionate, reliable, motivated, or active? Write a list of traits that you wish to embody, and next to each trait, write one to three things that you can start doing today to align yourself with them. For example,

if you want to be a better listener, call a friend or family member to whom you typically don't give your full attention and offer them the gift of authentic listening.

9. We have all made mistakes. We all have regrets. It's up to us how much power we allow our pasts to have over us. Write a few affirmations that begin with, "I lovingly release _____ because I no longer need _____." "I let go of _____ because I have learned _____." "I forgive myself for _____. I forgive _____. It's safe for me to forgive."

10. How do you want to feel right now? Write one intention word on a piece of paper and why you want to experience that emotion. What does it represent to you, and how will it make you feel? Keep that piece of paper with you throughout your day, and do one thing to spark that emotion. For example, if you want to feel at ease because you're consumed in stress and worry, take a break from work and sit outside by a tree, plant, body of water, or in the sun. Sit for a few moments with your eyes closed and only focus on the feeling of ease. By carrying your intention word with you and taking steps to feel your desired emotions, you remind yourself of your power to create whatever state of being you want or need.

Put these mantras someplace that you can return to when you need reminders of how amazing and powerful you are.

CHAPTER 4
GRATITUDE AND WISDOM

Dear Reader,

Every single day of our lives, we learn something. It might not be the grandest lesson that flips our worlds upside down and catapults us into action. It might not force us to stare our truth directly in the eyes. And it might not present itself as a lesson until months or years later. Nevertheless, we still stretch and grow every day.

Whether we're trying something new after years of doing the same thing, picking up the pieces of a broken relationship, or simply trying to make it through the week, we gain new insight from every daily doing and interaction. This accumulates over time to wisdom that helps us live with more presence, purpose, and gratitude.

Gratitude and wisdom go hand in hand. The more we experience, the more lessons we learn, and the more wisdom we collect. All of this leads to more gratitude for having the opportunity to live.

This chapter covers some of the lessons I've learned over the years that have not only altered the trajectory of my life but changed me as a human being. I hope you find a piece of yourself here.

Sending love always,
DANIELLE

How Did You Get to Where You Are?

D o you ever stop and think about how you got to where you are?

I went for a run recently and thought about all the tasks on my to-do list. There were ten things that I had to complete for my job and five personal projects. Whenever my mind mulls over daily goals, I become tense and fidgety, like everything must get done at the speed of lightning.

Then, like clockwork, my mind pushes forward into hypotheticals:

"If only I were (insert your dream job and life here), I wouldn't feel this way. Things would be so much easier if that were my life already!"

Then I thought about my current circumstances and what things were like for me five years ago. Before I became the director of an alternative high school, I was freelance writing and working in the restaurant industry. I was hired to teach a writing class through a connection with a friend who got me the job. That same friend recommended me for the position of director a few months later. The growth that I've experienced as both teacher and director has taught me a great deal about what it means to be a leader and an authentic human being. It's altered my perspective of the education system and opened my eyes to the power of our youth.

Then I thought about my apartment and how I wouldn't have found the perfect home for myself if it weren't for knowing the tenant who lived there before me. My apartment is my oasis and friends and family who visit ask how I scored such a sweet home for an amazing price. Living alone has taught me self-discipline, determination, and self-love.

Lastly, I thought of how much time I've spent writing posts and creating content for my blog over the years. During some of that time, I feared my efforts never "paying off" (whatever that phrase means, anyway). However, those blog posts and small daily efforts are now the foundation of this book.

When you believe that your happiness exists at a later date, you rob yourself of *your* story, this moment, your past and present efforts, and the magic that exists in each stage of your journey. You don't know who or what in your life now is the catalyst for your life's grandest accomplishments.

If, at some point prior, you couldn't imagine being who and where you are now, what does that mean for who you'll be and what you'll be doing a year from now? Five years? Ten years? Remember how a younger version of yourself would be *thrilled* to see the life you currently live.

When you release control, let go, and simply trust that everything is working in your favor, that what's for you can never miss you, and that you're exactly where you're meant to be, life will be more enjoyable.

Cultivate faith and know that your life *will* be better than you can ever imagine.

It's all up to you and how you see it.

How are you choosing to see it?

THE THING ABOUT
HEARTBREAK

The thing about heartbreak is that nothing can prepare you for it. There's no road map to tell you where to start and where you'll end. There are no directions to follow; no hand to hold; no sense of when things will get better.

The thing about losing someone is that you begin not to trust yourself. Your head becomes crowded with doubts—all the should haves, could haves, and what ifs. Nothing feels safe, secure, or familiar anymore.

They don't tell you growing up that enduring a heartbreak is like walking into the fire with your eyes wide open. There's nothing to shield you, no barriers or blockades to raise. All you have is yourself and the beating of your tired heart.

The thing about mourning is that it treads in both ripples and tidal waves. You could be standing in line at the grocery store, talking with a friend, or reading a book, and out of nowhere, your heart stops beating, your body heats, and fear seizes your veins.

The thing about being alone again is that you'll make discoveries each day. Some reap awareness; some garner ache; some even lead you into the dark underbelly. But all are meant to be.

What I wish someone would have told me is that even in moments when your world seems to crumble around you, even when you can't find the words to describe your current state, even when the dreaded night comes, there's a light at the end of this thing. Through this darkness, you're sustaining unimaginable growth.

Heartbreak, my dear, is not a path to be rushed but a trail to be walked. Observe the wildflowers. Take in the champagne clouds. Watch the sparrow bending midair. Breathe in yet another new season. This life is not meant to be linear; rather, its nature is of crests, surges, tides, and swells.

Learn to swim with it rather than against it. Become one with its unpredictability. Understand its constant changes.

When you allow the water to run, you purify yourself of all that needed cleansing.

CONNECT BOTH WORLDS

What has heartbreak taught you? What is your current heartache teaching you? How can you be present with your pain?

Close your eyes and take a deep breath. Place one hand on your heart and the other on your forehead. Create a bridge for your heart and mind. Connect both worlds. Try to quiet the analytical, thinking mind that puts labels and judgments on our emotions. Let yourself feel with your heart.

Say the following to yourself or aloud: *I love you and am always here for you. This is only temporary. This will soon pass. I will sit with you and love you wherever you are. It is safe for you to feel what you're feeling. I love you no matter what the circumstances are. You are my friend and supporter. Thank you for the opportunity to heal.*

ALL OF THIS IS PERFECT

I would tell you to run, to discover new terrain to unravel, but maybe you need to stay put.

I would encourage you to go out there and learn more about yourself, but there's wisdom in stillness.

I would urge you to spend your one precious life breathing in all that's new, exciting, and refreshing, but the old, outdated, and worn have their treasures, too.

I should have told you to follow your heart, even when it feels like an uncomfortable decision.

I should have told you that it's okay not to know. *It's okay.*

I should have reminded you that all is happening exactly as it's supposed to. You're not making mistakes.

I could offer you advice. I could tell you which way to go, but you've already heard me. You're free to choose.

I could tell you that you're wasting your time — not doing enough, giving more than receiving, loving more than accepting, hurting more than happy—but you need to learn this, my dear.

I want to tell you that there's more than this. In your wildest dreams, you couldn't imagine how happy you could be. But in growth and time, you will meet your bliss.

I hope you live this life in all its glory. The sun will shine on the base of your back, and rain will wash over you. Revel in both, my love.

I hope you choose your heart.

I hope you listen to the stirrings of your spirit.

I hope you find in others what you're seeking in yourself.

I hope you see yourself in your search to be seen by others.

I hope you know that all of this is perfect.

MAKING YOUR LIFE YOUR HOME

D o you ever think about the energy of a space? How it's not only the people who inhabit a room or a home that bring it life? Take, for instance, my current writing view. I'm sitting in my living room and to my right is the front door. On the back of the door is a coat hanger with a collection of jackets, hats, umbrellas, and bags. On the floor to the left of the door is my boyfriend's brown leather shoes. Underneath them is a small, reversible area rug.

To some, these are just things—garments we use to decorate ourselves or items we grab when running out the door to shield us from falling rain. But when looking at them now, I see the Yankees hat my boyfriend often wears on Sunday mornings when we make our iced coffee run up the block to the local bakery. I see the gray and white spotted umbrella that I was excited to purchase but spilled cabernet on later that day. The hat that my boyfriend tells me I look like an aviator in and the black jacket he throws on when going golfing in the fall.

It sounds simple in some ways. A person's belongings naturally have meaning and memories embedded within them. Still, sometimes it's looking at these items in such a way that reminds me of the intricate details of my life—the aureate lining bridled to my everyday existence. These items have made our first apartment a cozy home, each one imbued with the characteristics and habits of who we are.

I think about when we first moved into this apartment and how barren and open it was. How each week, we hung another frame, housed another plant, threw a new patterned pillow on the couch, arranged more dahlias for the kitchen table, and purchased an assortment of wine for the bar cart. This space was stripped of its former memories when we first got the keys. Now the walls are brimming with relics from trips overseas, local artisan's paintings, garage sale treasures, friends' drawings, a mirror we argued over, and recollections of time spent digging into the depths of each other.

A space can just be a space. A room can just be a room. An apartment can just be an apartment. A house can just be a house. It's how you choose to see your everyday surroundings that make your life your home.

This slender alteration of viewpoints make the space I rise and sleep in the harvest to my crop, the plants to my seeds, the love to my being, and the blessings that remind me of how grateful I am to have this one treasured life.

LOVINGLY IN BETWEEN

How often do you find yourself happy with where you are? I mean, *really happy* with yourself, relationships, work, and the day-to-day world. When you're in a space of non-judgment and acceptance of all things.

How often do you remain in the present moment without wanting or needing to be anywhere or with anyone else?

We often talk about living in the present and enjoying our current self and surroundings, but how many of us do that?

We spend so much of our lives waiting for some future version of ourselves. We're always wanting to be slightly different, rid ourselves of "negative" qualities, and get over our issues so we can be healed and renewed. But do we ever take the time to see what blessings this current version of ourselves is offering us?

What if we honored this space right now, as much as we praise the people we wish to become?

I've been thinking about this lately as I judge myself for accepting who I am.

Who am I right now?

I am both the seeker of liberation and the pioneer of connection.

I long for adventure yet my heart is pulling me inward.

I crave soulful interactions yet find myself settling for less.

I strive to be better every day but still indulge in laziness.

I want more personal success yet spend my time engaging in habits that don't serve that pursuit.

I love my alone time but can still feel lonely.

I want more time for myself, yet I fill my schedule with time for others.

I explore pleasure in all its guises yet discontent often follows.

I trust in myself yet have difficulty trusting others.

I want something hard to explain yet is completely describable.

I know change is inevitable, yet my fear wants to keep me constrained.

I'm in between two worlds. One keeps me safe, guarded, and forever protected. My fear rules this world.

The other is of great transformation, growth, and awakening. My heart governs this world.

I don't need to be confined to just one or the other. I don't need to judge myself for placing a foot in both landscapes. I'm free to flow within and without my own inner worlds.

I'm free to be me, exactly as I am now.

A woman neither here nor there but lovingly in between.

THE BALANCING ACT

Who are you now? What landscapes are you placing both feet in? Are you okay with the in-between?

Write your own list of contradictions and as you write them, cultivate unconditional love for wherever you are.

We're always in a state of change and transition.

We're always searching for something more.

We're always lovingly in between two places.

WHAT SONG ARE YOU SINGING?

When I was a kid, summer was my favorite season. I remember being around six or seven and getting so excited for the first warm day of spring that I would ask my mom to gather my bins of summer clothes from our crawl space so I could wear this one nightgown that I loved. (Apparently, I only wore this nightgown in the summer).

This little nightgown was more of an enlarged short-sleeved shirt with the Disney princess Belle on the front. It represented a changing of seasons, a welcoming of warmth, and dreamy June nights. I loved opening my windows on those summer nights and feeling a balmy breeze while falling asleep.

I was a little girl who loved to dream of all things enchanted, and those summer evenings alone in my pink room adorned with painted wall flowers, princesses, and stuffed animals was my haven—the space where I was free to be myself and dream as big as I could.

I think there's some old home video of my parents sneaking upstairs and filming me singing Disney songs to the night sky through the crack in my door. Yup, I was that kind of kid.

I've always been fascinated with the bewitching and mysterious side of life. I like to believe in the possibility of mystical encounters. Even to this day, I often view the world with child-like eyes and trust that anything is possible.

But there are times when doubt creeps in, and false

logic rules my brain, times when I ask myself: *Who do you think you are? Your dreams are too big. You're crazy for believing in yourself. You're not good enough.*

Are you familiar with this voice? Of course, yours would most likely offer a different set of criticisms, but nonetheless, we all have that berating voice in our heads that likes to put us down and make us feel worthless.

What happened from childhood to adulthood when we not only developed this negative perspective but chose to listen to it? Why does our criticism tend to outweigh our compliments? Why do we focus on insecurities rather than believe in our capabilities?

I have such profound moments of liberation where I know in my heart that I'm going to accomplish my dreams. It's so real I could taste it. But the moments when I doubt myself feel just as real as the moments when I lift myself up.

I want to be the little girl who didn't have a fearful thought in her mind. I want to believe in myself and my dreams *all the time*, not just in the quiet of the morning or the late hours of the night. I want my willpower, drive, and ambition to override any hesitation or uncertainty.

I want this, and I know I need this to live the life of my dreams. The next time I feel any pinch of doubt or pang of fear, I will remember the girl who couldn't wait to pull out her nightgown in early May so she could sit by her windowsill and sing because she wanted to.

Where is your heart these days?

Where can you dream more?

What song do you want to sing?

Whatever it is, go sing it.

Sing it with everything you have inside.

CALLING ON YOUR INNER CHILD

What were you like as a kid?

What did you dream about throughout your childhood?

What's your favorite thing about your younger self?

Where in your life can you bring in the energy of your inner child?

How will your child-like perspective and energy infuse your present-day world with more magic and wonder?

What activities can you do to help you tap into your inner child and invite them into your everyday world?

Life is more fun when we can view the world with child-like eyes. Challenge yourself to do one thing a day that a younger version of yourself would be proud of you for. Take a long nap. Play a sport or game just for fun. Take a leisurely lunch break outdoors. Play a joke on someone. Read a fantasy book. Go outside in nature and stand in awe of the magnificence of our natural world.

The more lighthearted you are, the more you ease into the present moment, and the more enjoyable life becomes.

RISING AND FALLING THROUGHOUT YOUR DAY

How many times do you rise and fall throughout your day?

I was looking back through a recent journal and noticed how often I experience such highs and lows throughout a single day. I usually write down everything I did and felt at the end of the day, including highlights and lessons.

When I looked at my notes, I was surprised at how often I've felt anxious, sad, or unmotivated, and how often those emotions were followed by spontaneity, laughter, hope, or vice versa. I went back and forth between the two, like a ball ricocheting, as though its nature were to bounce between opposing worlds.

I don't mean that I constantly go from sad to happy, anxious to upbeat, and negative to positive throughout the day, but I travel through varying emotions in just a few hours.

I can wake up in a great mood, get triggered, become frustrated, and raise my vibration. Then focus on everything that's working, become aggravated, feel anxious, and rise again. As I was reading through past journal entries, I started judging myself.

Wow. You're crazy, huh?

How erratic have you become?

Strapping yourself in for a rollercoaster ride of emotions every day, I see.

We can judge ourselves for the flux of emotions we

were born equipped to experience, or we can become the observer and simply observe.

It's not about being happy, grateful, and "perfect" all the time, but allowing yourself to dip into your shadows and then returning to your center of peace—whenever you feel ready to. You don't need to judge yourself for every moment you fall out of alignment with who you want to be and what you want to experience.

It's okay to stand between both worlds.

It's okay to feel sad.

It's okay to be uneasy.

It's okay not to always know where you're headed.

It's okay.

Remember, you can always bring yourself back to love and peace whenever you need to, however many times you have to, as long as you're here and breathing.

HONOR THE BEAUTY OF YOURSELF IN BLOOM

I was scrolling back through my Instagram feed recently and began cringing.

There were numerous grammatical errors in most posts, a handful of ghastly filters, selfies that I must have thought looked good at the time, and larger-than-life eyebrows.

Yup. Those feathery and unkempt eyebrows that I loved with all my heart, defended to my sisters, who told me that I needed to invest in a tweezer or threading session, the Brooke Shields-inspired duo...those bad boys. They were humungous in some photos. I felt my jaw hit my chest in shock at one photo in particular.

Then, I noticed some personal facts and stories that I shared about myself a few years ago, revealing the depths of my thought processes on a sensitive subject.

Did I really tell people that?

Why did I share such intricate details of my life as though I were placing a naked photo of myself on display?

God, I should delete these, shouldn't I?

I sat in bed with flushed cheeks and giggled. Life is funny when you can laugh at yourself and not take everything so seriously.

I fumbled with the idea of deleting three or four exceptionally embarrassing posts. I held my thumb over the "Delete" button and pondered it some more.

This is part of your history and growth, Danielle. Why would you delete a version of yourself that respected and honored this expression at a previous point in time? Don't you want to see your progression? Don't you want your readers to witness how far a person can come when they commit themselves to a goal?

I removed my finger from the trigger and decided not to delete the photos. As awkward as some of those posts are, they're essentially a large part of who I am now. I preach to my creative writing students to write in their journals every day to track their growth over time and have time capsules to explore at a later date.

How lovely it is to stumble upon younger versions of yourself, setting out to discover who you are while trying to make sense of the world around you. Deleting those posts is like ripping a page out of my journal—something I would never do now.

When I went through my first heartbreak, I threw out three full journals about the boy who broke my heart. I didn't want to identify with the girl who was so depressed in those notebooks. She was embarrassing to me at the time. How could she let someone make her miserable for months?

So, one day, I took those journals to the garbage can on the side of my house and happily dumped them straight to the bottom of the bin for pick up the following day.

It kills me now to think of those words gone forever, never to be picked up and read again. Pieces of myself that I poured into poetry, song lyrics, and reflections, most likely in a landfill or at the bottom of the ocean.

It's easy to look forward to the potential of who you can become. It's even easier to celebrate who you are now when reflecting on where you came from. But never mistake your current landscape as superior to your previous ones, for those rocky bluffs and jagged peaks were the catalyst for who you are today.

Don't mistake the journey for something shameful or embarrassing. Instead, honor yourself for the inclines you ascended when you didn't know what laid beyond the crest.

Where you stand now will be miles behind the terrain you walk in a year from now.

These steps are just as important as your future ones.

Your past and present moments deserve your love and attention, too.

Don't rush or regret the process.

Bask in the glory of your becoming.

Honor the beauty of yourself in bloom.

THIS IS THE SEASON
OF MY BECOMING

S ometimes, I catch myself drifting into daydreams, where I envision the perfect partner, an ideal life, and the warmth of being held by someone who truly understands me.

I see myself writing at an antique desk with a cup of coffee in hand on a cold winter morning. I look out to a large canopy of trees and the sun glistening off the lake behind them. As I create worlds within worlds on my keyboard, I feel arms wrap around my shoulders like a long-awaited embrace.

This is home. This is what I've been waiting for.

I see the fern and emerald shades of the mighty oaks and pines. I smell the frozen lake, tranquil and hushed in her piercing beauty. I hear the robin and kestrel nestling deeper into their humble refuges. I feel comfort knowing that I've found the person who sees me in all of my imperfections and cradles the fragility of flawed love.

My mind travels to this world in moments where I seek more than what I already possess. It is the dream my mind has come to believe as home.

What is home now, though? Where do I retreat when no hands are coasting the length of my back or eyes peering into mine?

I think of how this solitude may be one of the last times of my life that I'm truly alone. For this is indeed the first time that I'm experiencing seclusion this way.

As my heart longs to love and be loved, I see how my

struggle to fulfill my desires has built strength as solid as stone. When the moon is the only light I can see, and my body craves the heat of another, I remember how I've learned the greatest freedom in autonomy. I remind myself that I'll miss this version of my life when my love comes along. I'll remember how I dreamt of steadfast commitment but wish that I adored my own company more.

This is the season of my becoming.

This is nightfall before daisies bloom.

This is where I'll meet myself, greet myself, and love myself.

This is where it begins.

LIVING FOR THE WEEKDAYS

W hen I was a little girl, my bedroom was next to my parents on the first floor of our blue-gray house with the tiny glaucous rocks in the driveway. I remember hearing my dad get up for work most mornings at 5 a.m. He had the same thirty-minute routine each day: shower, blow-dry his hair, spray hairspray, put on his watch, splash cologne on his neck, grab his keys, wallet, and any spare change off the top of his dresser, and plant a kiss my mom's forehead while she was still sleeping.

Some mornings, when I heard the shower turn on, I'd get out of bed with Teddy, my teddy bear, and RaRa, my old yellow blanket, and with eyes half-closed, I'd hop into bed with my mom.

My dad frequently went on business trips, so my sister and I took turns sleeping in our parents' room until he came home. There was an inherent comfort to crawling into warm sheets and snuggling up with mom. I loved those mornings — the coziness of falling back to sleep to the sounds of gentle breathing.

When my dad got ready for work in the mornings, I looked forward to waking up to the smell of his cologne or the sound of his keys. Those mornings I'd receive a kiss on my forehead, too, as he'd whisper, *I love you*, before leaving for work.

My dad worked hard for our family and did his best to ensure my sisters and I had an exceptional childhood full of fun family trips, bountiful Christmas mornings, memorable birthday parties, and family dinners around the table every night. He always made sure to let us know how much he loved us.

When he'd arrive home from work, my sister and I would hear his car door shut and run to the front door to greet him with open arms and smiles from ear to ear. I remember how much this meant to my dad — to come home to two daughters who were elated to see him.

As time went on and my sister and I got older, our race to the front door became less frequent, as we'd discovered shows like *Boy Meets World*, *Sabrina the Teenage Witch*, and *Full House*. I remember one day when my mom asked my sister and me to run to the front door to greet dad because it was his favorite time of day.

It was only until I got older that I realized my dad's unhappiness with his job. Although he was a hardworking and successful businessman who rarely ever took a sick day and worked to his best ability, he didn't enjoy his work. He did what he had to do for his family, but his job took a toll on him.

It took me years later to understand how something as simple as rushing to the front door to greet and hug him would mean the world to him. This small yet significant act of stopping what we were doing to say hello gave his life more meaning.

I'm grateful that I had an amazing childhood with wonderful parents who always loved and supported me, but I often think of my father's relationship with his job and how I don't want to repeat that pattern. I don't want to go to a job that I dread every day. I don't want to fear the Monday to Friday routine so that I can live on Saturdays and Sundays. I don't want to rush my life for an imagined and relaxed future.

Why does retirement get to be the "best" years of our lives? Why can't we have some form of that now, even if that means choosing a job that sustains and fulfills us in this moment of our lives?

Most people settle for jobs they dislike (or mostly hate) to pay for their home, cars, bills, necessities, and life in general, but rarely do people think about their state of happiness *while* they're living.

Why don't we ask ourselves these questions more often?

Why don't we make a map of our goals and figure out reasonable ways that we can accomplish them without believing our work has to be dreadful?

Why don't we put our happiness first?

Why don't we dare to dream?

I understand that each person's situation is different, and it's not always as simple as it sounds. Still, if we took just fifteen-to-thirty-minutes a day to develop a plan for what would make us more fulfilled, we'd proactively take steps toward a more meaningful existence.

Monday to Friday is our life, too. It's not just the weekends, vacations, and retirement that we should live for.

So, my question for you today is, what is your dream?

What would make you the happiest?

What can you start doing today that will benefit you today and tomorrow?

What do your desires look like?

ALLOW YOURSELF TO DREAM

Write these questions on a piece of paper and connect to your heart when writing your answers. Record yourself speaking your answers aloud. Listen to your recordings while getting ready in the morning, driving to work, or falling asleep at night. Make copies of your answers and tape them around the most-visited parts of your home—your bathroom mirrors, the refrigerator, your nightstand, inside your closet, or on your front door. Remind yourself what you're living for and how you want to feel *while* living.

I believe if you allow yourself to dream, you begin to grow your best possible life.

The life that's destined for you.

The life you were born to live.

LOVE THE PROCESS

Have you ever felt like something wasn't right for you, but you continued to pursue it? You knew deep in your bones that there would be no happy, forever ending. You knew that things would eventually change one day—hearts would be broken, and opposite paths walked. But you still chose to stay, to see what could come of it.

Maybe you feared the sadness that would dawn if you broke things off before something triggered you. Even the relationships that aren't for us still hold a place in our hearts. We still miss people when they're no longer in our lives.

Why is that, though? Why is it when we know we want more, when we understand that something is missing, when there's this silent yet urgent voice in the back of our minds pushing us toward the unknown, we still choose to stay? Why is the comfortable more appealing than the undiscovered, solitary path? Why do we have to dread heartbreak and loneliness when we know it's the only escape from a relationship we're not happy with?

There have been many times in my life when I've mulled over the idea of leaving a past boyfriend because nothing was necessarily wrong, but everything wasn't *right*. I've always found that to be the hardest situation to remove myself from because I was giving up something secure and familiar and, in most cases, that made me happy, but just not as happy as I knew I could or wanted to be. And there was always that second voice asking me if I'd ever find what I was looking for when I finally left.

It feels easier to walk away from someone who's betrayed

your trust, lied to you, or proved you right for having suspicions about them because there's always that anger to hold on to—the resentment that fuels your independence and sparks fires of change.

Those precise situations of my life have been some of the most revealing and satisfying. How empowering is it to reclaim your freedom and face the unknown with bravery so vast it encompasses the whole of you? How interesting is it to watch yourself unfold in beautiful shapes and forms you wouldn't have experienced if it weren't for your undoing?

I've learned that it's not only the moments when we place one foot after the other where the most learning occurs. There's value in the space of no longer wanting to be in a relationship and not being ready to leave. We must respect and honor that space as much as the part of ourselves that's brave enough to make the fearful change.

If you think about it, what would this life be if we didn't experience the in-between? How would our lives look if we left a situation when we thought we could be happier elsewhere? What would it feel like to always act on the warring voices inside our minds without taking the time to be present with all that currently is—even if your current scenery looks different than how you desire it to be?

Honor the space you're in with the respect and admiration that a thirteen-year-old version of yourself would have for the life you're now living. Let go of believing that things need to be a certain way because you've decided they have to be that way.

When you can learn to love the process without always rushing toward the result, then even your uncertainty becomes a sanctuary to dwell in.

Revel in this, in all that is.

All of your moments deserve to be loved.

MY WORKSPACE

Sometimes my workspace is messy. Sometimes it's neat. Some mornings there's steam from hot coffee misting in the air. Some nights there are remnants of chocolate cake on an antique plate in the corner.

Most days, I love arriving at this space. My desk is where I feel closest to myself. This is where I make sense of things. It's in this little corner of my bedroom where I'm most connected to my dreams, and the more I show up to this space, the more it shows up for me.

There are days when I sit for hours and only put a few words onto the page. There are times when I can't stop my hands from dancing across the keyboard, when my fingers race to catch up with the stream of thoughts I'm pouring into them.

My desk is my happy place. It's home. It's never let me down, and it's funny because as I'm typing this, I realize that I created this space. Essentially, I feel the happiest when I'm here by myself.

Most days, when I place my joy in external sources and a future my mind conceives to be better than my present, I'm reminded that my contentment is a result of personal effort. Of harnessing my energy, shifting my perspective, and believing in what's not yet tangible.

My desk symbolizes hope, dedication, creativity, discipline, fortitude, and determination.

It's here that I meet myself.

It's here that I continue to rise to the occasion.

It's here that I journey for more.

It's here that I birth my dreams to life.

CREATING YOUR OWN WORKSPACE

When creating your workspace, design it with your dreams and aspirations in mind. What lights you up? What gets you excited? What makes you feel like you're capable of achieving anything you put your mind to? Create vision boards or collages with inspirational photos and quotes that remind you of your dreams. Write your top five to ten goals and place them where you can see them. Frame photos of yourself with family and friends who are your greatest supporters. Put your favorite pens in a jar, display your favorite books on your desk, and burn a candle to help set the mood. Include anything and everything that helps motivate you to continue working toward your dreams. Creating a beautiful workspace makes the process more fun and rewarding!

THE SPIRIT THAT BREATHED YOU INTO BEING

I'm trying to trust the timing of my life. I understand that I long to be twenty steps ahead most days and often want to rush my dreams, but I'm also aware that I sometimes stand in grace and am happy where I am.

There are times that I imagine complete focus, total sobriety, and full dedication. Then, there are days that I'm pulled into a tide of reckless abandonment, self-destruction, and the pursuit of unadulterated freedom.

Some nights I think of you and crave your arms around my waist, your warm breath on my neck, and your voice against my ears, but most nights, I find comfort in the solitude, peace among the quiet, and fulfillment in the vacant space beside me.

I've discovered that I'll always want to be somewhere different from where I am. I'm in a perpetual state of transition. Once I've reached the plateau of my desires, there will be another set of wishes I aspire to pursue.

I have one foot in the ethers and the other grounded here. My heart is with you, and it's also my own again. My dreams are within arm's reach, but I still stretch for what lies beneath them. I believe in myself, but sometimes doubt overwhelms me.

It's okay to be in both spaces. It's okay to know and then not know. It's okay to remember and then forget again. We were born all-knowing, all-powerful, and all-encompassing, but we weren't meant to recognize this right away.

Your life, this existence here, your constant journeying for more, the sky you soar and the soil you trudge, the simplicity that visits you followed by the dark night, the total bliss and the plummeting sadness—all of it—is meant for you.

You came here for this. Do you remember? Can you see? I know you imagine a perfect life, but this moment you're living right now is just that. Please try to remember that even in your pain and confusion, you once asked for this.

Close your eyes and look within...
for the spirit that breathed you into being,
the soul that chose this path,
the light that is your home.

FULL CIRCLE
MOMENTS

Full circle moments. I think about them a lot. When I moved into my first apartment alone, I loved having a space that was entirely my own. No roommates. No pets. Just me, myself, and I. I woke up and felt pride and accomplishment as I thought about where I was just a year prior.

February of 2019 marked the beginning stages of one of the biggest changes in my life and little did I know that I was about to embark on a journey that would teach me the most about myself. There was so much confusion, doubt, and unease then. I remember waking up most days with a giant pit in my stomach, asking any being higher than myself to guide me and offer insight into what my next steps should be.

A year into living on my own, I remember sitting on my couch and looking around the walls brimmed with my chosen artwork, the bookshelves with my favorite reads, the plants I situated to garner the most sunlight, and the home I created for myself. If you were to tell the past version of me that in just one year, I'd experience the most growth of my life, learn to love myself more than I ever imagined, cultivate and harness creativity daily, and manifest a living space that reflects who I am, I wouldn't have believed you. I couldn't see beyond what was in front of me.

We do this often, don't we? We only perceive what's visible—what's standing directly before us. We mull in our doubt and have trouble locating the clarity at the center of any blackout. We don't always lift our gaze to see the potential of what our lives can become—of what we can become—when we give into love rather than fear, positivity rather than adversity, and strength rather than instability.

When you look closely, though, you'll see that where you're standing now is a full-circle moment from where you were just a year or more ago. When you look even closer, you'll realize that some time from now, another full-circle moment will occur—one that *you* will have created.

Look at the growth you've already endured and think of how much you'll progress when you allow yourself to flourish.

WHEN TO LISTEN TO YOUR GUT

Have you ever stayed in something when you knew it wasn't right for you?

Have you ever ignored your gut when you knew you should be heading toward the unknown?

Have you ever looked back with regret and asked yourself, *Why didn't I trust myself?*

These situations are merely part of the human experience. I believe that specific people or experiences walk into our lives so we can exercise the muscle of listening to our gut instincts.

You know what I'm talking about...the person you had an inkling was not entirely all they made themselves out to be. The ex-boyfriend or girlfriend that you thought wasn't completely honest. The job that you stayed in when you knew there was a better opportunity waiting for you elsewhere.

It's usually only when we come out of these situations that we kick ourselves for not listening to our inner voice that already knew the truth.

We're magnificent beings with an inner well of wisdom rooted in the depths of the universe. Yet, we don't normally tap into that source of knowingness when we're desperately looking for answers.

I don't know why it's so hard to trust ourselves. Nine times out of ten, our gut feelings are not only correct but spot on. Yet even when we know this, we tend to ignore our voice because what's comfortable is more appealing than moving forward into the unknown.

When our gut speaks the loudest, necessary change is approaching. Our guidance system always seeks to align ourselves with the highest possible truth and love. It's never steering us toward anything that isn't meant for us.

I've started looking for small signs that push me further along my path to self-trust and reliance. We live in a mysterious universe where if you ask for something, you'll receive an answer. You just have to be open and receptive to spotting the clues.

Lately, if I'm looking for clarification or confirmation for something, I simply ask the universe my question and then go about my day, trusting that I'll receive the answer. And you know what? I always get a reply. It may not be big, bold, and directly in front of my face, but I observe my surroundings, notice possible connections, and realize that coincidences are not always coincidences.

The more I believe that I live in a supportive and loving universe, the more I trust my decisions and heart.

Don't shrink into what feels safe if your heart pushes you toward a new adventure.

We can spend our whole lives circling in routines that feel safe yet don't ignite the passion we're searching for. You know the truth by how it feels to *you*.

How does your truth feel? How do you listen to it? What steps can you take to bring you closer to your truth? Are you heeding the signs? Are you connecting the dots and spotting the clues?

I promise that if you ask for what you're searching for and believe that it's possible for you, you *will* get a response.

Journal Prompts for Recognizing Growth

- How has your past helped shape who you are today? Include specific moments from your past as reference points for your personal changes.
- Remember a challenging time from your past and how you felt while going through it. How has your perspective altered from then to now? Are there any benefits you reaped from that time of your life?
- What are you proud of yourself for overcoming? How did you overcome that hardship, and why do you feel proud of yourself for handling it the way you did?
- What's something you accomplished or overcame in the last month that surprised you? What about the experience or your behavior surprised you the most, and why?
- If your past self were to look at your life right now, what would they be the most excited to experience?
- If your future self were to offer you advice right now, what would they tell you?
- If you could tell your past and future selves one thing each, what would you say?
- Where in your life are you not listening to your gut instincts? How does it feel to ignore your intuition? How would it feel to take divinely-inspired action based on your gut instincts?

- If you have a desk, altar, or personal space in your home that you've dedicated to your spiritual practices and dreams, what can you add to it that's missing from your current mindset? If you don't have a desk, altar, or personal space, how can you create one? What would you add to it? (Photos, quotes, vision boards, statues, candles, inspirational visuals, etc.).
- What wisdom and insight are you currently collecting from your relationships, work, and the day-to-day world? How is that wisdom and insight helping you see yourself and your life differently?

CHAPTER 5
OUT OF THE DARKNESS, INTO THE LIGHT

Dear Reader,

I used to be afraid of the heartache that comes with change. In some ways, I still am. As humans, we're wired to want consistency and familiarity. Change can inconvenience our daily schedules, lifestyles, and emotions. If something disrupts our natural flow of life, we feel lost and unsure of what steps to take next.

It's precisely in the moments when you're not grounded that you grow the most. It's only through becoming uncomfortable that we expand our comfort zones, and there's so much you can learn from allowing yourself to live in the in-between.

Most people avoid the discomfort that comes from change, and consequently, they stay in jobs, experiences, and relationships that aren't fulfilling. Leaving the comfortable is frightening but cultivating the bravery to face your fears and land on the other side of them is where authentic and inspired living occurs.

No one said life was meant to be easy. From my own experience, it's the decisions that were the hardest to make, the relationships that broke my heart, and the total disarray that followed that brought the greatest gifts.

This chapter is inspired by those difficult choices, for they became the gateway to my freedom, happiness, and peace.

Sending love always,
DANIELLE

SEASONS OF ME

As a little girl, I'd wander through my backyard as though I were an explorer, peeking under fallen leaves for evidence of miniature life. I'd put on my raincoat and boots on a drizzly spring afternoon and set out to discover families of snails contently trailing along in their daily quests. The few trees in my yard were a forest to me then, and no matter how many times I'd venture out for new revelations, I'd always come across magic in my pursuit of other worlds.

Summer arrived, and I was fifteen, looking in the mirror and counting all the ways I didn't measure up to the girls around me. My journeying through soil and roots was now bypassed with a desire to be seen by others.

When fall settled, I felt your hands glide up and down my legs, your breath in my hair, and your mouth everywhere. You told me you loved me with closed eyes and sweaty palms. After, I laid my head on your chest and wondered if you meant it.

I came to meet myself in December with the first snowfall of winter. I cozied up in our home, watching as the grass became a white sheet. You sat in the chair in the corner of our living room. I waited for you to look over at me. You did, but you didn't see me. I told myself by this time next year, I won't be living here.

It's now somewhere between seasons. I'm finding my way back to the girl who was mystified by nature, in tune with her surroundings, and enamored with her world. She understands her cycles; she knows when it's time to venture outdoors and the moments she must retreat within. She knows herself from previous seasons of not knowing herself and doing whatever she could to recapture the woman inside.

I wonder what this next season will bring, the people I'll meet, the cities I'll visit, and the different women I'll become. I hope to continue this way, welcoming the unknown, seeking alchemy in what's around me, letting others inch closer toward me, and reinventing the person I'm always becoming.

Rhythms and revolutions are the nature of my being. I stand grounded in my ever-evolving unfolding.

CHRONOLOGIZE YOUR LIFE LESSONS

What are some of the rhythms and revolutions of *your* being? At what points in your life have you grown—in the most expected and unexpected ways? What have you learned from these turning points, and how have you changed due to them? Grab a piece of paper and write down your answers. You can also experiment with a poem that follows a similar layout, starting with the oldest version of yourself and chronologically moving forward until you reach the end of the poem, which represents who you are now. These types of poems are some of my favorites to write!

It Was the Way He Understood Me

He made me feel like the only woman in the room. I'd look at him from across a crowded party, waiting for his eyes to meet mine, to feel that warm sense of recognition hit just the right spaces within me.

He knew the words that would penetrate my soul. He knew the corners of my back, where his hands would coast and land at exactly the perfect spot. He understood me the way birds know rain is nearing; how a tree senses growth in its limbs when warmth arrives.

At first, I never noticed how easy it was for him to catch a woman's full attention; how his natural movements triggered awareness and attraction from those around him. Once I saw the varied shades of blue, hazel, and brown cast upon him, I felt a longing to hold him closer and a desire to run.

How could someone spark the wildest fire I'd ever felt yet know the fastest way to extinguish it? He didn't need to do or say anything to dim its blaze; all it took was watching and observing him to see how easily he could destroy me. This wanton destruction pulled me in like a moth nearing its demise as it flies toward the flame.

I don't know how many times I rose to my death in my pursuit of him, but I know the mountains and hills that multiplied within me were seeded by the man I held both tightly in my grip and let loose for fear of drowning.

You see, it's not that I won't open the gate for you

to enter my house. This doorway's been closed for so long that its guardian has forgotten where she left the key.

WHEN YOUR HEART
SOUNDS DIFFERENT
THAN YOUR MIND

He told me that he could picture us getting married one day. He brushed his beard against my cheek, his wet lips grazing my ear, and smiled as he said it. We were sitting intertwined on his black leather couch after we got home from a friend's birthday party. He had drunk quite a bit throughout the night—a few Johnnie Walker Blacks neat. I could tell he was feeling more relaxed and happier than usual.

I laughed it off and didn't take it too seriously. We had been dating for almost two years, and I wasn't trying to make any sudden, big moves just yet. To be honest, I wasn't even sure if he was my "forever" guy. I was also always skeptical of marriage. I'm content just being with someone. I don't need a piece of paper to validate that commitment; my heart and words affirm my intent.

I knew what I loved about him: the way he would let his guard down and laugh from the bottom of his stomach, his unwavering generosity with everyone he met, and the rare look I received when he thought of how lucky he was to have me. But I was even more sure of the things that concerned me: his inability to match my desire for deep, meaningful conversation, how his money brought him his only sense of self-worth, and how I sometimes felt invisible and lonely around him.

For a while, I had been blindsided by the adventure money can bring. Lavish dinners with expensive champagne, spontaneous getaways overseas, unexpected gifts after fights, and the grand surprises for holidays and birthdays. As exciting as all of that was at the time, there was always this underlying complacency and overarching feeling that things weren't enough. I didn't know what my *enough* was, but I kept searching for it in him, knowing fully well I would never find it. My heart longed for the love he couldn't give me, and a spark I kept hoping would suddenly appear.

Yet, when he said he could picture us getting married one day, his words still offered some warmth, some false idea that *maybe this could work out in the long run*. (Insert montage of a small wedding, romantic honeymoon, nights out with friends, trips to Europe, and endless surprise gifts).

For brief moments when things were going well between us, I chose to believe in this future version of us. This go-to reel my mind would play after a great night out together or during one of his genuine, deep belly laughs didn't include the gap lurking between us. The ample space that stood between being a couple now and married forever.

There was always this flip-flop of emotions I was juggling. In the rarer instances, I imagined an unrealistic, happy future together. More frequently, I'd sit next to him watching TV and wonder when my last time sitting on that couch would be. I was enacting a script that was bound to end with a breakup, but still hoping the writer would scribble in some last-minute edits or the leading male role would have a major shift in character. I was the definition of the blind leading the blind, except I knew what it was like to see.

The night we broke up, I remember standing in his doorway and hugging him with more emotion and affection than we ever shared during our two years together. I left his house, drove straight home, crawled into bed, and cried until I fell asleep. I only remembered our sweet moments and the qualities I loved about him. I kept replaying the romanticized version of us and didn't allow my mind to drift to the moments of doubt and confusion.

When I woke up the next morning, I kept thinking: *This is it. It finally happened, like you knew it would.* Yet I still did not believe it. The overwhelming sadness I felt the night before was lightly threaded with a sprouting sense of freedom and optimism for the new. It was just a seed at that point, but I knew it would eventually grow into something better and more suitable for me. I guiltily checked my phone to see if I had any missed calls or texts from him, hoping that his name would be lit in a rectangular box on the screen. But neither of us reached out in the middle of the night.

Entertaining my heartache, I opened my photos and scrolled through our two-year history together. Weekend getaways, small daily highlights, celebrations with family and friends, intimate moments with just the two of us, and I saw that even in our "best" times, I still wasn't as happy as I could be. Each photo displayed the better moments of our relationship, but also a girl who wanted something more. I always knew that there was something else waiting for me; I just had to be ready to move on.

The last photo I looked at before turning off my phone was of us at a Fleetwood Mac concert. I was leaning back into his chest, he was kissing my cheek, we were laughing, and I thought to myself, *If it's possible to love someone when you know it's not right, how much better will it feel when the right one comes along?*

HOW I LEARNED TO
POSITIVELY COPE
WITH TRUST ISSUES

I used to label myself as someone with trust issues. I'd replay my life's script. It began with witnessing infidelity as a child, evolved into dating cheaters as a teen, and culminated in seeking out deception in my twenties.

I never realized it at the time, but I placed a large portion of my identity into this idea of falsehood. I not only investigated the possibility of betrayal; I expected it to be part of my experience. I put so much effort into thinking, writing, and speaking about the inevitability of infidelity that I became a spokesperson for it. I put all my faith into the very thing I feared the most.

I was infidelity's handmaiden, yet at the same time, a preacher of the aphorisms, "What you are seeking is seeking you," "Like attracts like," and "What you put out, you receive." My whole energetic vortex, my aura, my karmic vitality, if you will, were orbiting around the theme of, "All men are the same," "People ultimately can't be trusted," and "The law of attraction is real!" No wonder I was inviting people into my life that proved exactly what I wanted to see—solely what I was *trying* to see.

Suffice it to say, it took me over ten years to figure that out. To finally lift the veil from my eyes and understand that if I believe myself to be a victim of distrust, that is undoubtedly who I'm going to be. The choice was mine.

The freedom was mine. But I kept choosing to remain in the prison I had happily built for myself.

I allowed my thoughts to wander to imagined scenarios of unfaithfulness with every detail perfectly illustrated. I thought rummaging through my partner's phone every once in a while was understandable and necessary in ensuring everything was still "okay." I had knots in my stomach when my respective other had a guy's night out or a boys' trip. I'd recount the stories I heard from friends about their boyfriends cheating on them at bachelor parties. And I'd remember how eighty percent of the married men I met while bartending feigned singlehood.

It's easy to play into this belief of adultery being the norm. Most of what we see on TV and in movies involve glorified affairs. E! News doesn't rush to cover wedding anniversaries and loyal commitments. Radio shows exploit women who catch their boyfriends or husbands buying flowers for their mistresses and not for them. I think, in some ways, we're a society obsessed with duplicity.

This is clearly no way to live. It's easy to believe in the collapse of your valued treasures, but it's harder and more beneficial to place faith in what your life will become when you let go of fear. And quite frankly, it feels better to trust in the timing of your life and believe that where you are, who you're with, and what you're doing is meant for you. There's no naivety in that either, but rather gallantry. Instead of buying into what most people believe, you're carving your path by elevating your expectations.

I realized that I wanted loyalty rather than skepticism and a relationship that supports me rather than wears me down with doubt. I always knew I wanted those things; I just didn't know how to act as though I did. I thought I was doing that by "telling it how it is," but I was only setting myself up for the next chapter of my already exhausted story.

I've learned that what we focus on most, we receive. We create our stories. We may not have control over everything that happens to us, but we choose how we feel in any circumstance. We can run in circles repeating the same old script or choose a new path, an awakened way of living and trust in *ourselves*.

Have faith, cultivate self-reliance, and rest assured knowing that your one cherished life is worth trusting.

TRANSFORMING YOUR WEAKNESSES INTO YOUR STRENGTHS

Where in your life have you struggled with something that was hard to get over? Did you self-sabotage and spend your time focusing on that issue? Did you mull over everything you disliked about your problem, yourself, others, or the world without taking the time to understand yourself and why you felt the way you did?

Whenever we're going through a challenge, our first instinct is to avoid it and run in the other direction. Instead, we should walk toward it to understand it more clearly. The only way we know ourselves better is by tending to our wounds and not being afraid of what makes us uncomfortable.

Make a list of your fears, anxieties, and self-created problems. Then write a list of how you've self-sabotaged and believed that life was out to get you due to those problems. Is there a pattern in how you choose to deal with your issues? Do you notice that you've cut yourself off from people or experiences that trigger emotions out of fear of feeling them? Have you expected the worst for yourself and consequently experienced a string of unfortunate events?

We grow only by recognizing our weaknesses and choosing to deal with them rather than run from them. Now that you have your list of challenges and your *old* coping mechanisms, what are some healthier options for responding? How would these options be better for you now and in the long run? How do you think you'll feel in six months or a year from now if you choose healthier habits today?

A DELICATE DANCE

He tells me he loves me with his eyes. He doesn't say it for reciprocation or to make a grand gesture, he just wants to share what's in his heart.

I've never met someone like him before. He's grounded yet fragile and sometimes looks at me as though I'm strong enough to break him.

It's funny how you could be both the wave and the shore, the hail and the soil, the storm and the peaceful aftermath. It's interesting how we're often perceived as one or the other, never two in the same.

Sometimes I think we just want to be swept away and the one sweeping. It's a delicate relationship, our dance with infatuation and fear.

How does he do it? Make these movements that once weighed me down seem so light and free?

Maybe it's because he's seen more than the others. Maybe he's felt beyond what my history was capable of grasping.

And within that knowing brings a tenderness I've not yet discovered. A flame not yet flickering. An enchantment not yet matured.

How does he do it, you may ask?

By calming the once shaken mind into serenity, shifting the former distrust into hopeful faith, and making what used to feel ordinary beautiful.

WHEN THINGS FEEL HARD TO HANDLE

I'm in what some people call a dark night of the soul or what others, in plainer terms, call a funk, deep sadness, or simply a hard time. For someone who prides herself on being upbeat, optimistic, and inspired by life, I haven't felt in tune with that woman lately, and I'm patiently waiting for her to return to me.

I tend to wake up excited for the day, grateful to be pursuing my passion, and living a life I'm proud of. I understand that it's both a blessing and a choice to live in this manner, except I haven't been able to bring myself to feel that way again.

There's a heavy blanket resting on me when I wake, weighing me down. As much as I try to remove it, I'm still defeated.

It's just another cycle of life that I'm becoming accustomed to. I know this won't last forever, and I trust that all is working for my highest good, but even with that awareness, there's still uncertainty. I preach being present in all of life's moments — the happy and the sad, the easy and the difficult, the love and the heartbreak—but lately, my mind only focuses on the finish line. The moment I'll be free from this.

As much as I want liberation, my heart is complacent in its ache. A welcome sign leads me into the darkness, a chair to sit in for a while, and a bed to rest my head for the night. This sadness is as much of a comfort to me as my desire to be released from it.

In my heartache, there are memories, and memories are what my mind holds on to. If this anguish leaves me, then so will my history, and I'm not ready to let go of it.

We're meant to grieve, cry, and not always feel our best.

We're meant for this because we grow in this space.

This is where we meet ourselves and rise to our highest potential.

Even though it's dusk, we learn to breathe in light.

BREATHE

Take a moment to sit with yourself, wherever you are, with whatever's on your heart. Close your eyes, place your hands on your heart, and sit with yourself for a few moments. Love yourself for who you are and where you are in your life right now.

LET GO OF FEAR AND
TRUST YOURSELF

As we get older, time feels like it's moving faster with each passing day. Since the nature of time is swift and fleeting, we don't often realize how long we stay in patterns, relationships, jobs, or circumstances that we've outgrown.

We like to remain in our comfort zones because comfort equals security, and security is "safe." Our world won't flip upside down at any random moment because we're sticking to the normal routine of things. Normalcy offers momentary happiness when choosing the traditional over the unexplored.

What is true happiness, though, when your mind drifts to daydreams of a different kind of life? What is real comfort when you'd prefer an elevated existence—a more loving partner, a job that gives you purpose, and a world you're excited to dive into every morning?

Time plays a major factor in our lives because we tend to think that we have more of it than we do, so when we're unsatisfied with something but are afraid to make changes, we tell ourselves that we'll eventually rip off the band-aid and move forward, but just *not yet*.

We'll wait until we feel ready to take the plunge.

And so, we wait, and wait and wait.

Months pass, years pass, and any time we say we'll finally break free from what no longer serves us, we make excuses for the timing not being right. Whether there's an upcoming birthday, holiday, trip, event, or simply a week where we'd prefer not to deal with the pain that comes from making necessary but sorrowful change, we sit tight and continue waiting some more.

How much of our lives do we spend waiting?

How much of our existence do we put on hold until we live?

I've done this many times throughout my life. I guess you could say I'm well versed in the art of lingering.

Lingering until something better comes along. Lingering until the change miraculously happens on its own. Lingering until I've been worn down and have no other option but to face darkness.

And so, I did.

I chose the path of pain to feel what my heart had longed for. What my soul had been pushing me toward. What every fiber of my being was inching me into.

I caught glimpses of my new life when I was still stagnant and terrified of moving. It revealed itself like snow drifting from the sky at dawn. It came to me like a warm breeze wandering off ocean waves. It welcomed me into its world in moments where I couldn't imagine any relief.

I knew it was real because I could taste its sweetness. I understood that it was calling for me because I could hear it beckoning. I recognized its embrace because it felt like home.

Once I knew in my heart that there was a new life waiting for me, that my visions weren't the result of complacency or delusion, I realized that I had to call upon strength I'd never felt before. I'd have to remember fortitude when panic ensued and begged me to return to what was. I'd have to remind myself why I left in the first place and that there was no security in what I was leaving behind.

I never imagined I'd be as happy and fulfilled as I am on my own. I used to place my contentment in others, and I'd search for the missing pieces within me in partners, friends, lovers, and jobs, and none of them ever fully fit. I believed that to be whole, I had to share my life with someone or something else, and it was only after I treaded through sacred suffering that I met myself. Now, the light radiating on me is more resplendent than I'd ever envisioned.

If you're reading this and are a fellow lingerer like I was, I hope you sit with yourself and the visions that come to you like cool, restoring winds after a fierce thunderstorm. I hope you know that you are worthy and deserving of a life beyond your wildest dreams. I hope you listen to the yearnings within you and understand that they're whispering divine messages to lead you where you're meant to be. I hope you know that it's okay to desire a new a life but not feel ready to part ways with the old. I hope you know that you are always loved, supported, and held in your own warmth.

I hope you take a chance on yourself.

I hope you choose yourself.

I hope you build your own paradise.

VISION BOARDING

Can you make a vision board of where you want to be in the future?

This can be in a month, two months, six months, a year, or two years into the future—whatever timeline you're looking to work with.

Grab a blank piece of paper or poster board and create a collage of images, words, art, quotes, old photographs, and mementos that remind you of where you want to be. Place the vision board somewhere in your bedroom where you'll see it every day. Whenever you look at it, cultivate feelings of thanks and trust that your dreams *will* come true.

Remember where you're heading.

And remind yourself that it's okay to be standing where you are now.

GRACE IS IN EVERYTHING

My family recently came across some news that changed our perception of life quite literally in the blink of an eye. My oldest sister was diagnosed with an aggressive form of breast cancer, and just like that, our reality was flipped upside down. What we once held close in the palms of our hands drifted further away from us. Certainty was replaced by ambiguity, and the assurance of life continuing as it always has no longer felt like a luxury.

This is what happens when someone close to you is going through the most challenging season of their life—a season immersed with heavy storms that worsen before the sky sees any clearing. It's more burdensome when you can do nothing to stop it in its tracks, alter its course, and send it the other way. You begin wishing that the bruised blue of the clouds above and the whipping of wind circling midair were heading for you instead. If only you could grab hold of the pain and keep it for yourself, to stop others from hurting—wouldn't it be easier for everyone? You can handle it. No one else needs to carry this.

Life can seem cruel and unforgiving at times, can't it? How interesting this existence is. Sometimes you can't help but wonder why things are the way they are. Life is already hard enough as it is some days. How much more can we possibly endure?

The truth is as much as we only like to believe in love, we are by nature a mix of darker elements too. Without pain, there's no relief; without sadness, there's no joy; and without death, there's no life. We're comprised of light and dark, and we exist *because* of that duality. One of the most remarkable aspects of being human is our ability to rise after falling and believe in something we can't see but feel in our hearts. From our sorrow, doubt, and confusion, we garner the miraculous traits of faith, hope, and resilience.

Life may seem harsh and ruthless at times, but let's not forget that it's because of these experiences that we meet the potential of our souls. We learn the most about ourselves when we meet our darkness. What we often look past and ignore most days rises to the surface and asks us to look deeper, to feel fiercely, and to love harder despite all calamities.

Even our most tumultuous seasons offer peace. This journeying of being human is not so that we can feel perpetual contentment and greet the easy and expected. We are here waking and sleeping, rising and falling, loving and enduring, every single day so that our vulnerability births clarity and our weakness bears strength. The two are one and the same, forever swimming in unison throughout the trajectory of our lives.

If you're finding yourself in a hard season, please remember this:

You've proven to yourself that you can make it through any storm. You're the one who put yourself to sleep and rose again to see the birth of another new day. You're the one who pushed yourself into the world when you didn't want to get out of bed.

You're capable of handling anything. It's this precise moment of doubt and fear that you'll look back on at some future date and see blessings rather than sadness, hope rather than disdain, and lessons rather than bewilderment.

There's grace in everything. You just need to remember to look for it, even when standing under heavy clouds.

BE PRESENT WITH YOUR PAIN

Wherever you are, find a space to close your eyes, place one hand on your stomach and the other on your heart, and breathe.

There's no need to force your pain away. You don't need to run from your discomfort. Instead, sit in recognition of your capacity to feel deeply, strongly, and vulnerably. Honor your strength in handling challenges. Send love to the parts of yourself that want to give up. Believe in your resilience. Listen to *all* the voices within you.

Where there is weakness, there is strength.

Where there is doubt, there is hope.

Where there is fear, there is fortitude.

Where there is loss, there is love.

Take a deep breath. Hold your breath. Release your breath.

Repeat this as many times as you need to until you feel a greater sense of calm.

TODAY, I CHOOSE ME

I've been thinking about relationships lately, as I'm choosing to be alone for the first time in almost ten years.

It's freeing, this feeling of needing no one but myself—of wanting nothing but solitude. How easy it is to get consumed in someone else, their life, and the possibilities of what you two can create together.

When things don't go according to either of your plans, though, you're back at square one, and soon enough, you begin the search for someone else to fill the void. It's this never-ending cycle of always wanting or needing someone by your side, and to be released from this habituation has offered me many awakenings.

I look back at my past experiences in love, and I see a girl who I don't recognize anymore.

A girl who:

Craves attention.

Desires intimacy even when followed by emptiness.

Encounters the promiscuous yet knows commitment.

Struggles to be seen but never truly sees herself.

Repeats cycles that pick her apart and leave her wounded.

Chases after men who don't value or respect her.

Stays in situations far longer than she should.

Denies her intuition, even when it shouts for her attention.

Settles for the love that she thinks she deserves.

I've been all these girls and more.

I've fallen in love far too many times to count, and

often, I was seeing men through the lens of who they could be, rather than who they were. I've stayed in relationships that I knew from the start were never going to work but was hopeful that maybe one day they would. I believed in men who, at my deepest core, I didn't trust, who made me think I was crazy for ever assuming they betrayed me, to discover that the voice telling me to run was the voice of truth.

I settled, even when not treated with respect.

I loved, even to my detriment.

I tried, as hard as I could, for as long as possible, until I couldn't anymore.

I've also experienced love that greeted me with warmth, listening, understanding, and the comfort of feeling at home.

But today, for the first time in a long time, I'm not choosing anyone else. I'm not looking to fill any gaps. I don't need anyone to "see" me.

I see me.

I trust in me.

I love me.

I choose me.

GROWING PAINS

When I was an early teen, I used to think that I wasn't lovable. I had this inherent belief that I wasn't worthy of total, unadulterated love.

Self-worth was a battleground for me, a constant fight to prove to others and myself that I had something beautiful inside of me, just as the other girls around me so effortlessly possessed something beautiful inside of them.

I remember many mornings getting ready for school and carefully applying concealer to broken-out skin. A new pimple emerged every day, and a deeper well of self-consciousness grew with each outbreak. I based so much of my self-worth on the state of my complexion that instead of listening to what others said when they spoke to me, I'd follow their eyes to see if they were observing my breakouts.

I'd look at other girls who never had to deal with acne at such a young age and become envious, wishing I could swap lives with them. I thought they must have it so easy—going through life with flawless skin. Most nights, I'd pray for my acne to disappear by the time I woke up, offering God a lifetime of dutiful service for clear skin.

I won't yell at my parents anymore if you get rid of this zit!

I'll do better in school and take on extracurricular assignments if you can heal my skin!

I'll go to church every Sunday and listen to the priest's sermons if you remove all my pimples by 7 a.m. tomorrow!

Obviously, that bargaining didn't work out in my favor. So, my backup plan was to cultivate poise and attraction in school by using humor to make others like me. Don't get me wrong, I enjoyed my teenage years, but before I reached high school, middle school was a special kind of torture. Between enduring severe breakouts for the first time in my life, losing friends who were my closest allies, and feeling the pressures of trying alcohol and drugs, middle school was its own purgatory.

But on a random Wednesday in the 8th grade, I met a boy who didn't seem to notice the same appearance I did when I looked in the mirror. He was tall with dirty blonde hair and ocean blue eyes. He liked bands I'd never heard of before, like Arcade Fire, Modest Mouse, Wilco, and The Wrens. He was creative and artistic and believed in anarchy (which I didn't understand but thought was incredibly cool). He went everywhere on his skateboard (which I grew to believe was the best way to get around). And he showed me documentaries on extraterrestrial life, ancient civilizations, and secret operations covered up by the FBI.

He was the type of person who introduced me to new worlds I'd never experienced before, and I couldn't get enough of him. He made me feel beautiful and seen, and I began to understand what falling in love could do to a person.

I fell asleep smiling with excitement for the following day, to be able to see him in school and talk about things I never discussed with friends, like the possibility of aliens roaming the earth or how a nihilist and believer were so compatible with each other. I woke up in the morning and felt pretty; rather than focusing on my flaws, I daydreamed about the weekend, when we could hang out in his backyard or at a park and meet his friends at parties who also only wore black, spiked their hair, and chose skateboarding as their primary source of transit.

I had a boyfriend! My very first boyfriend. I wanted to showcase our love to prove that I, too, could be accepted, welcomed, and admired. I, too, could be loved. Life was the sweetest it had ever been for me at the time. I never knew how happy I could feel.

As the months passed, I began placing a large portion of my identity into my relationship with Nate, and I lost myself in him. Anywhere he stood, I was beside him. I wanted to talk to him throughout every hour of the day, and since texting and calling on cell phones was a new thing, I savored our endless conversations over the phone or in person. If we weren't talking or together, I felt this ache of needing to be closer to him.

I wasn't my own person anymore. The girl who longed to be accepted and seen was now addicted to the high that a first love can bring.

If I didn't hear from him for a few hours, I began thinking something was wrong. Maybe he didn't like me anymore. Maybe he was getting tired of me. Maybe he finally saw me for who I really was—undeserving and incapable of being loved.

At around four months into our relationship, we went from seeing and talking to each other every day to making plans only once every other weekend and talking just a few times during the week. When I saw him in school, there was a growing distance between us that felt more friendly than romantic. I panicked inside. I had constant knots in my stomach and was unable to eat, sleep, or focus on school.

What was happening? It was only a few weeks prior that we couldn't get enough of each other, or I couldn't get enough of him. What happened to him not being able to get enough of me? Was it something I said? Was I too clingy? Was he not attracted to me anymore? Was he ever?

The questions and uncertainties that rolled through my brain made me feel helpless and paralyzed. It was my first time in love. It was the first time someone had ever chosen me. It was the first time I ever felt the nauseating pain of realizing that the box I had placed all my happiness in might be taken away at any moment.

I didn't even want to approach Nate and ask if something was wrong because I couldn't face the truth. Part of me knew if I asked him what was going on, I would have to meet my heartache, and I wasn't ready for depression to completely settle in. I forced myself to move through my days as though there was a permanent dusk. I battled my anxieties and convinced myself to believe that everything would be okay. I would be okay. I just had to wait and hope that Nate would return to us.

But, as I'm sure you already know, that didn't happen. As I knew it wouldn't, too.

When we finally broke up, there was no clear communication on our ending. We just gradually stopped talking, or rather, Nate cut all ties with me. I didn't have the courage to ask him what was going on. I just watched from a distance as our relationship dwindled and died.

It's interesting how so many of our early experiences in life shape our identities in some way or another. It's funny how something that happened in our youth can still affect us years later.

I recently felt insecure and wondered if the love I seek will ever find me. Will I ever be seen?

Those old feelings of unworthiness rose to the surface. I remembered the girl who wanted so desperately to be loved, who fought for acceptance outside of herself because she believed she wasn't lovable, even by herself.

This is the first time in many years that I'm alone and choosing to be so, with no distractions, no partners, no flings—just me. Within this seclusion comes power, insight, and the occasional loneliness.

Now that it's almost two decades later, I no longer look to others to fill the void I sometimes feel. I no longer place my happiness, identity, and self-worth in someone else. I no longer seek externally for what I already possess within.

Life comes full circle. As I'm alone again for the first time in ten years, I've come a long way from the girl who fought to be seen by others, loved by others, and chosen by others.

I love me, and I'm grateful to meet myself again.

ONE DAY

O ne day it will happen for you. You'll walk into some coffee shop or bookstore and see him. You'll catch each other's eyes and shy away for a moment, looking down to the ground or next to you, then glance up once more to see if his eyes are still on yours. They will be, and you'll smile. His face will brighten and blush, and all within that second of seeing fate in a stranger, your day, your world, is forever changed.

How does it happen that at just the precise moment you breeze through the doorway, it's as though the universe conspired a slight nudging of his head for him to look for you?

Your mind flashes forward to your first night together. How his lips will taste. What his hands running along the base of your back will rouse. The kinds of conversations you'll have until dawn awakens. And all within a single glance, you've created a world within worlds that has not yet blossomed.

But you hope it will.

And you wonder if he, too, is seeing the colors you've painted, the walls you've built, the flowers in bloom, and you hope that he is because if he is, then maybe you're no longer waiting.

CLEARER VISION

It was one of those things where you just knew. You knew in the buried abyss of your gut that something was exactly how you thought it was despite the denials of its existence. You knew the irrefutable awareness that came rising like ocean water over your head, then back down again, affording you clearer vision and the ability to see what you already knew you knew.

It's within that rooted knowledge of the truth where the line between understanding and suspicion grows very thin. I understood it in how they looked at each other, their eyes meeting just long enough to say what their mouths couldn't. A slight flicker of her eyelid, a glance backward at the curls of her hair, and a tension that filled the room.

I suspected that I was the only person to see their rituals, their exchanges, the ever-mysterious nature of their relationship. I felt us dwindling away and watched the girl I wanted to be disappear from view.

Who did I want to be? I wanted to be calm and confident, wholly unwavering and unconcerned. Beckon a tidal wave my way. Pull out your sharpest weapons. Tell me the harrowing truth of it all. I'm like stone. I can stand it.

Oh, so there is something there between the two of you?

Oh, so I should simply get over it then?

All that I wanted to be was merely the result of what I needed to become to stay afloat on the drowning ship we were sailing. We were sinking slowly for so long that we barely realized how far under we'd gone. How much deeper was I willing to let myself go? How many deafening signs advising me to flee was I going to ignore in my descent into senselessness?

The truth is that you always know the truth. We can tip-toe around it, play hide and seek, and blatantly stare it down and ignore it. It will always resurface and plant itself into the tiny moments of our lives until we recognize it, though.

Because the truth is, I could have kept dancing in the entanglement of the web I found the three of us in. I could have played the role of bystander, watching the weekly performance continue, act after act. I could have kept feeling detached.

But I thought of this. What's worse? Being alone and lonely or feeling utterly alone with someone else?

SAD LOVE POEMS

You told me I write too many sad love poems. You said it in the tone I became accustomed to. The one that stretched a distance between us until I had discovered my own island, bountiful in seedlings and secure in her own company.

"Well, sometimes I feel sad," I'd reply.

I always needed to explain myself. I always demanded you to see. I'd pull out my map, and as the words fell from my lips, I began leading you into the mountains, alongside the sweet tulips florescent on the cliffside, onto the hidden passage, and up to the sovereign moon in all her loveliness.

As we stood on the edge of the bluff, hand in hand, below a sky illuminated with starlight, I realized you couldn't see what lay before you. We were two lovers from foreign lands, and I spoke in a dialect you couldn't comprehend. As much as we talked, you'd never understand me.

How couldn't you see that those poems I was writing were never about past lovers or remnants from last night's dreams, but was me trying to speak to you in a language I hoped only you could read?

But you weren't reading.

I was already gone.

THE WINDS ARE CALLING

I don't know myself anymore. Just last week, I was ready to take on the world with whoever stood by my side. I welcomed anyone who asked for me. Now, I can't seem to escape myself.

All I want is space.

All I crave is seclusion.

All I need is myself.

I'm being pulled up and away into something much bigger than me. I can't yet see the marvelous forces that are calling. I don't yet know where they may lead, but I've been waiting for this moment my whole life.

For the day where instead of being wrapped up in you, us, or the possibility of us, I focus my energy on me.

How many people can say their focus is themself? How many others dare to dream of an existence outside of the one they created? How many people dream?

At night, I stare at the moon, asking her to pull me close, transport me to where fantasy and reality meet. How I long for something more. How I wish to meet myself.

The winds are coming. I'm beckoning their call. I allow them to do with me as they will.

ONE TIDY SUM

I had been trying for a while to make myself believe that I was sincerely happy. All the pieces fit together to create a seemingly perfect whole. He was there; we spent our time together; we loved each other. Everything moved as steadily as it could except for some bumps along the way.

I really wanted it to be enough. I wanted to feel beautiful and elated when I was with him. I always hoped that he'd bring out the liberated girl in me. In the past, when I met her, I knew love was at its most palpable.

Love is tricky because sometimes what you think is "perfect" is like a package containing assembly instructions with a multitude of missing pieces. Some of what you need is there, some of what you want is missing, and the best you can do is stare at the guidebook to try and make it one tidy sum.

And sometimes, as hard as you try to make things work and hope that everything will eventually fall into place, it's only when things have been broken that you realize how imperfect it was.

You think of all the wrongs committed, the times you felt hurt and betrayed, what you wish you could go back and change. You try not to remember the good because it only draws you back in and interrogates you on why you're alone and whether you'll be okay on your own. Then loneliness comes knocking, and you're surrounded by a crowd of panicked thoughts demanding answers for your choices.

And you begin to wonder...are you truly lonely in the absence of damaged love, or are you just scared that you'll never find what you're looking for?

We're creatures of habit by prolonging the inevitable. It's harder when love is still present, but it's simply not working. It is easy to point the finger and place blame, to move on with anger for someone's wrongdoings instead of walking away with the simple realization that not everything's meant to last forever.

There's comfort in being alone, though. No one else can bring out the best or worst in you except yourself, and when you're alone, you tend to search for what's best in yourself again.

STRENGTH IN SOLITUDE

What are some of your favorite things about being alone?

What do you love to do during your alone time?

What lessons do you learn from being on your own?

How can you shift your perspective about solitude to be more positive?

Where can you make more time for yourself?

THE STORY OF MY FIRST HEARTBREAK

I was fourteen the first time someone broke my heart. I was lying lifelessly on the couch with mono when I received a large silky teddy bear from my lanky skater boyfriend, Nate. He had dropped by unannounced with this surprise, not expecting to see me twenty pounds lighter with a wet rag on my forehead and a voice like Kermit the Frog.

I didn't have the energy to care that he was seeing me like this. I thought I was hallucinating when a human-size teddy bear was placed under my arms to console me. I was alone and bedridden for almost four weeks without my parents' company and with no recovery in sight.

I remember watching TV with him and barely being able to make conversation because my throat was so swollen. Despite being in three-day-old clothes and smelling like a sewer, I still didn't want him to leave. He was the first boy I ever fell in love with. He was the reason I started writing love poems. He had taken me on my first real date. He was the beginning of my love story, and at the time, I wanted him to be my ending. Little did I know, our final chapter was coming faster than I could have anticipated.

After Nate left my house, I texted him on my new Razr flip phone, thanking him for the teddy bear and stopping by to visit. After hitting "Send," I fell asleep and woke up three hours later to no new messages. Another hour passed and then another until it was the next day, and I still hadn't heard from him.

I began to worry. Did my sick appearance so repulse him that he decided to call it quits? Wasn't he the one who gave me mono? How could he abandon me in my time of need? Didn't he care that he was the reason I was bedridden for a month?

Days passed, and then a week with no answer to my calls or texts. That's when the real sickness occurred. The kissing disease crept out of my esophagus, crawled into my head, and infected my brain. I began formulating a list of explanations for his absence.

Maybe he was abducted by aliens! He does love the idea of life on other planets.

Maybe the government got to him! He was a proud anarchist, after all.

Maybe he's on an impromptu family trip and forgot his phone at home. Silly Nate!

No, I got it! He's finally writing that book he's been talking about and has shut himself off from the world to focus! Yes, that must be it! My scholarly and motivated boyfriend!

When the sickness subsided and I could finally eat solid food again, my delusions disappeared. I learned that during my six-week infirmity, Nate had not been abducted by aliens or the government but had started dating someone else. Cue the melancholy sounds of a tiny violin, a cascade of tears, and the grim reality of my first heartbreak.

Ah, that summer was a sweet one. The beginning of June to the end of July had already been wasted to poor hygiene, liquid foods, and endless sleep. Thank you, Nate! Thank you, mono! (I did lose twenty pounds, though). The end of July to the beginning of September was occupied by heartache, loneliness, and the comfort of my journals. (This is where my love for writing began to flourish).

After our breakup, I filled three journals, beginning to end, with sad poetry and confessions of love and heartbreak. At that point, I had taught myself that the only person who could truly love me was me. Many loves will walk in and out of my life, but the love that remains is my love for myself.

I write this not only to share a comical and heartfelt story of my first heartbreak but to shed light on the process of life and the natural order of things. We have our highs, lows, the ordinary, and the in-between, but we also have unremitting resilience. At some point or another, we'll be able to look back on what we're going through with laughter, a sense of gratitude for all that we've learned, and a hopeful perspective for more lessons to come our way.

CULTIVATING A LIGHTHEARTED PERSPECTIVE

What was one of the most challenging experiences you went through as a teenager? Can you go back in time and vividly remember how you felt when enduring a challenge you never thought you'd get through? Can you identify the feelings of isolation, fear, and mistrust from the new experience? Can you find the humor in it now that you're on the other side of hardship? Can you laugh at what once felt like your entire world crashing around you?

How can you apply that same lighthearted perspective to your current journey? Where in your life do you take yourself too seriously? How does incorporating a humorous perspective balance your heavier emotions?

It's okay to feel the heaviness of life. Hold as much as you can carry for as long as you need to. Remember, though, what feels like an excessive load today will one day be as light as a feather. By remembering that you'll eventually look back on your life with a loving perspective—maybe even a humorous one—you can welcome the balancing act. It all comes back to stability. Tapping into the density of your emotions while observing them from an outsider's perspective enables you to see things more clearly. By seeing yourself and the situation more clearly, you can respond to it in healthier ways.

LOOKING AWAY

Where do you go? he asked. *When your eyes move to the window and your gaze off mine?*

I couldn't tell him what I was thinking. How one day I'd have to leave him because of all the times he abandoned me. How he made promises he had no intention of keeping. How he expected me to stay when he had already fled.

I couldn't bear to face the truth of how I was planning my escape. For the day where he'd break one more promise and hurt me one last time, so I could muster the strength to finally walk out the door. To leave him waiting like he had me do for so many years.

Now I look truth in its eyes. I'm no longer afraid to see.

The only time you saw me was when I was looking away.

The only time you cared was when I was already gone.

NATURE'S UNDOING

Nature had taught her everything she knew, and when she needed to learn it again, she ventured into the wilderness and listened. Trees harbored secrets that passing winds could whisper. Dawn's rising shed light onto pathways that trailed into the wise woods. A single starling's flight led the sequestered route. Insects crawling through soil showed the intricacy of meager life.

She, too, at times, felt tenuous, but she knew what it was like to live loud and without concern. Like the hurricane heading toward her, she was a primitive force, reckless and untamed, ready to be drenched in the cold, renewing rain.

Nature constantly replenishes and recycles. Everything has its season. Nothing is permanent, yet everything remains.

She wouldn't be alone in the forest forever. She knew to wait for the earth's ceiling to open. To pursue refuge in sundown. To summon all the coyotes and wolves.

Through her undoing and the beckoning of the wild within, she will meet herself.

The land there is untouched, pure, and lucent, as she too will be again.

ALLOWING YOURSELF
TO FEEL DISCOMFORT
MEDITATION

> Listen to this meditation on **Struck Inside Out**'s *website. See "Additional Resources" at the end of the book for the link to access it.*

This meditation will begin with a small journal reading and end with breathwork to help you process your emotions. It will support you in finding peace with your current state of being. I hope this is a calming session for you.

I am trying to honor this space in my life where I don't feel like myself. Most days, I wake up to an anxious pit in my stomach that tightens with each breath and broadens with each flicker of my eyelids. It twists and turns until I lay in bed for a while longer, waiting for the uneasiness to subside.

I am so used to labeling myself as someone happy, optimistic, and excited about life that when I feel the opposite, I believe there must be something wrong with me.

I find myself fighting against the winter storms that wrestle within, the tide that comes in high, and the night sky that waits for dawn to return.

I can never sit with my shadows. I can never allow myself to be in pain. I am always trying to swim upstream and float above the waves crashing down on me. The harder I resist, the deeper I sink.

I fell asleep crying last night. I held my face in both hands as the tears flowed down my arms to my elbows until I couldn't hold myself up any longer. Until I struggled to breathe. It was the first time in months that I let myself feel loss; to grieve a life that is no longer mine; to miss someone I love.

How long have I been drifting asleep?

I allow the waters to flood. I want to be swept into the eye of the storm. I am no longer afraid. My defenses are down. Life, please do with me as you will. Please teach me what I must learn. I will not hide from you any longer.

How often do we disregard uncomfortable emotions? How frequently do we run from our pain? Why is it difficult to sit in our discomfort and simply be in it?

Sometimes in our lives, we are nudged to beckon our unfolding. We are asked to let go, surrender, and relinquish all expectations of who we should be, how we should act, or what steps we should take next. A great mystery lies beyond what our eyes can see. A new life waits for us when we walk into the depths of the unknown.

Take a few moments to sit with yourself and whatever state of being you're in. Create space to welcome your discomfort. Invite your worries, stress, and fear into your heart. It's okay to experience these emotions that we label "bad" or "wrong."

You are human. You are allowed to feel everything, both good and bad, and light and dark. We are here to feel *all* that we can. Take this time to simply feel.

Allow yourself to be as you are.

Take a few deep breaths.

Breathe in through your nose, creating space for your pain. Exhale deeply through your mouth.

Take another deep inhale through your nose. Breathe in your current state of being.

Exhale deeply through your mouth.

Do this three more times at your own pace.

Say the following statements to yourself or aloud:

It is okay for me to experience all the emotions housed within me.

I love and accept where I am in my life right now.

I love and accept myself.

I am a beautiful being with the capacity to grow and expand.

What I'm feeling now won't last forever. It is only temporary.

I welcome the unknown. I embrace darkness. It is through this darkness that I step into the light.

I am allowed to flow within and without my inner worlds. I am free to be me as I am now.

Before we close this session, place both hands on your heart and hold yourself for a moment longer.

This is the current moment of your life.

Your next steps may be unknown. You may not be able to see the road ahead. But all you must do is be with yourself *exactly* as you are. *Lovingly* as you are. *Perfectly* as you are.

Cultivate gratitude for being able to feel so profoundly.

You are beautiful as you are right now.

I send you love and blessings.

May you stand forever guided in your truth.

JOURNAL PROMPTS FOR FOLLOWING YOUR FEELINGS

- How did it feel to sit with your current state of being?
- What emotions came forward during your meditation, and how did you initially respond to them?
- Do you feel safe allowing yourself to experience discomfort? Why or why not?
- Did your discomfort offer you messages during your meditation? What were those messages, and how do you feel about them?
- What visions presented themselves to you, and what do you think they represent?
- Do you feel lighter or more resistant after offering yourself permission to feel your pain? Why do you think you feel this way?
- If you're resistant to letting yourself feel discomfort, what is one small thing you can do to feel more comfortable doing so? (For example, breath work, physical movement, journaling, talking with a therapist, recording yourself speaking lovingly to yourself, or writing a letter to your fear).
- What are three benefits of allowing yourself to feel your emotions?
- What are three disadvantages of cutting yourself off from your emotions?

- If your present self were to send you one piece of advice for your current emotional state, what would you say?

CHAPTER 6
LETTERS TO THE
GIRLS I'VE BEEN

Dear Reader,

I wrote this collection of letters after being inspired by Sara Bareilles' book, *Sounds Like Me*. In her memoir, she wrote beautiful, heartfelt letters to herself at different points of her life. I always loved the idea of writing letters to a past self from the perspective of who you are today, not only to tap into your history but to discover the wisdom learned over the years.

Letter writing is an excellent tool for understanding yourself better. I can't even count the number of times I've brought my pen to paper to begin this practice. What started as a prompt for testing my writing skills transformed into a therapeutic outlet for loving myself more.

This self has taught me forgiveness, kindness, understanding, and compassion. I learned not to take myself so seriously. I discovered how to laugh at my mistakes. I told myself I was sorry. I encouraged myself to believe in my dreams. I pushed myself to go after what my heart desires. I loved the darkest parts of me. I let myself be as I was, am, and will one day be.

Letter writing is most powerful when you're honest and vulnerable. When writing letters to your past, choose a time in your life that was hard for you to endure. Send love and encouragement to that self from the person you are today. When writing a letter to your present, focus on the areas of your life that are working and those that are a struggle. Shed light and encouragement on both aspects and remember to write from your heart. When writing a letter to your future, get specific about where you hope you'll be when you read your letter again.

Don't worry too much about grammar. Instead, focus on tuning into your truth. Express how you truly feel. Don't be afraid to go deep. These letters represent a sacred communication between you and your most authentic selves.

I hope that you return to this practice time and time again. It will help you appreciate your journey, honor your individual growth, and love yourself unconditionally.

Sending love always,
DANIELLE

BELONGING

Dear Danielle,

I've read your journals and see that you're having a hard time in school right now. Your group of friends is changing. I know that's scary for you. You crave security in your surroundings, but you're beginning to see this as a good thing because your new friends are awesome.

You're a big jokester in the seventh grade, and you like playing pranks on people after school. You bought three goldfish from the pet store up the block at Pet Palace and left them on Trevor's front doorstep with a forged note from his Grandma, saying, *Congratulations on your wonderful report card! Grandma is so proud of you!*

You couldn't stop laughing at the idea of ringing his doorbell and running, just to have Trevor open the door to see a bag of goldfish and a congratulatory note from his Grandma on his front stoop. After doing this a couple of times with your best friend, Sarah, Trevor invited you in to show off his growing aquarium, asking you to please stop giving him fish as gifts; he couldn't house any more in the tank he was forced to buy. He did end up naming all of them, though.

You like at least four different boys. There's Jay, who makes you laugh so hard you snort, but he's always staring at Lisa. There's Paul, who passes you notes in class, but the moment the bell rings, he's MIA. There's Andrew, the tall and muscular basketball player who could pass for a junior but has never given you a second glance. And there's Mark, who's sweet, goofy, and not the sharpest tool in the shed, but you believe he'd make a caring boyfriend. All you want is a boyfriend.

This part of your life isn't the easiest. You don't like how you look in the mirror, and you're constantly comparing yourself to other girls, measuring your self-worth against their mature appearances. You believe that to be beautiful, you must have clear skin, no visible pores, a growing chest, a plump bottom, and perfect teeth—all of which feel terribly out of reach for you.

Even though you landed on the "7th Grade Most Popular List," you were labeled as the girl with "no boobs, no ass, and oily skin." This makes you feel even more self-conscious than you usually do. You run to the bathroom at least once during each class to dab your skin with a tissue so no one can notice your oily complexion. Although you're admittedly honored to be considered popular, you wish every part of your body could morph into an unrealistic standard of beauty. You want to look different. You want to feel different. You want to be different.

Coming from the version of you who's now in her thirties, your skin type is something you become grateful for. More oil equals fewer wrinkles. And guess what? At thirty-two, people often mistake you for a twenty-five-year-old. How awesome is that?

Don't obsess too much over your skin. I promise, what you notice about your complexion, most people aren't seeing. Try your best to focus on the features you love about yourself and stop looking for new things to feel bad about. As you get older, you'll gradually become happier and more secure in your body, even though you feel behind in the race toward adulthood.

You worry that your entire grade is growing up faster than you are, and you wish life would slow down. You already feel like the good old days are behind you, and you frequently wish that you were born in another time period where flip phones, computers, MTV, and AOL didn't exist. New forms of technology seem to highlight your insecurities. If you text a boy and he doesn't reply, you think you did something wrong. If your friends have an AIM profile that doesn't include your name in their list of best friends, you feel like an outcast. If you're not up to date on the latest music videos on MTV, you must not have good taste in music.

You're an old soul who appreciates the little things, like the art of letter writing and calling someone's house phone to speak to them. Texting takes too long with having to hit each number multiple times to access the letter you need. Bleeping on Nextel phones is fun because it feels like you're using a walkie talky, but you also receive public voice messages at any hour of the day. And AOL chatrooms are admittedly exciting but now you and your sister fight for screen time on the shared family computer so you can gossip with friends.

Even though you're not ready to, you begin drinking with the rest of your friends. Your first drink is from the boxed white zinfandel in your parents' shed. When mom and dad go out to dinner at their favorite restaurant on Friday nights, you open the box and pour your friends a sample. You feel like the first sommelier in your class. You sip and smile, detecting everyone's initial reactions from above the rim of your red solo cup.

You'll start to expand your horizons and open your repertoire of alcoholic beverages, soon discovering the sweet taste of a two-day hangover from Jose Cuervo. Dad will film you throwing up into the toilet on your camcorder and leave it on your nightstand for your viewing pleasure the following morning. He hopes this makes you never want to drink again. He has high hopes.

You battle with feeling like you belong somewhere, with someone or something, and you fiercely want to be loved. The most beautiful thing about this time of your life is your discovery of writing. You see that you can give yourself the love you've been searching for through your creativity and passion. Your journals teach you to process your experiences, and your writing practice becomes a reliable companion you never knew you needed.

This birth of creativity will one day become the driving force of your life.

Keep going. Continue writing. It will get easier from here.

I love you, and you're perfect.

Love,
DANIELLE

FINDING SOLID GROUND

Dear Danielle,

It's the ninth grade, and you're nervous to begin at yet another new school with hundreds of new students. You don't want things to change, yet you don't want them to stay the same. You walk through the wide hallways and already imagine the day you'll graduate and move on from this place.

You fell in love with a boy and got your heart completely and utterly broken. That is after he gave you mono. You lost about twenty pounds and looked like a cast member of *Survivor*—not at the beginning of the show, though. People kept telling you to eat a steak, assuming you had an eating disorder, but you took this as a compliment, considering you always wanted to be thinner. Not being able to swallow for a couple of weeks just happened to do the trick, and fast.

Your heartbreak doesn't dissipate for quite some time, and you begin to believe that the old saying is true—that people really can die of a broken heart. Your only source of solace is writing in your journals, day after day, while listening to Norah Jones' *Come Away with Me* album, trying to mimic her sexy, sultry, and bluesy feel.

This is the time of your life when you'll find that you love writing more than anything else. Your journals are your most coveted possessions, and you look to them as friends with whom you can be your whole self.

Most of the ninth grade is about learning to be comfortable in your own skin, and I wish I could say this will get easier soon but hang in there a little longer. You have a couple of more years before you learn to love and embrace your weird, whimsical nature. Your eccentricity attracts you to your new best friends, so try to remain true to yourself.

The girls you surrounded yourself with for the past five years aren't as interested in you anymore, and you notice how you don't like yourself around them. You don't trust your instincts. You do things that you don't like doing, like smoking weed and then bugging out for hours. Yet, every time one of them mentions rolling a blunt with the group of guys you're always pairing up with, you still take a few hits, hoping that you'll see the same appeal they do. You never do.

Remember when you smoked at your friend Anna's party and thought her dog was talking to you about what life was like in her house? Or when you asked Jenn to call an ambulance because you could swear your heart was pounding out of your chest? Or the night you walked home from Mari's and believed your neighborhood was a movie set instead of real life?

This habit of always trying to fit in when circumstances don't feel right for you creates unwanted experiences. Like getting so drunk off Mike's Hard Lemonade and shots of Bacardi Limon that you make out with a guy you don't even like, and when his hands slip into your underwear, you don't say anything.

You drink to escape what you usually feel and step into someone you wish you were, but you always feel worse about yourself.

Ninth grade isn't all embarrassing and undesirable experiences, though. This is the year you form an alliance with Carter and Sarah, two friends who will be in your life until your thirties. The parts of yourself that you hid from your group of girlfriends, like your unhinged humor and intellectual nature, thrive under the influence of your new friends. The three of you are offbeat and unconventional. You can make a joke out of anything, and because of your ability to draw comedy from the soberest of situations, you attract a parade of characters into your weekend escapades.

Like the weekend you visit the notoriously haunted house up the block from mom and dad's because you hear live music blasting from its open windows. When you arrive at the front yard, you notice the door is open, so you walk the pathway toward the house to see what's inside.

A man with long dark hair and a beard sits on a beat-up polka dot couch, strumming a guitar. An obese man wearing a Led Zeppelin crop top and Ray-Bans plays the drums, and a woman with bleached blond hair wearing a bikini top and pink shorts rides a stationary bike with a microphone in her hand, singing in high-pitched tones.

They wave for you to come inside as you stumble in, buzzed and laughing. They continue performing as five of their friends stand around the living room with drinks in their hands, listening to their rendition of "Ramble On."

After listening to a few of their songs, the three of you snoop around the house to see what you only imagined before. Carter notices an open door to the basement, and all it takes is one unified glance to understand that you have no option but to venture downstairs.

When your feet hit the basement floor, you scan the room to take in its décor. There's a poster of Barbie holding a teacup that reads "Drink Tea with Me!" on a tie-dye painted wall. Chains and whips in a basket in the corner; a circular spinning bed with zebra print sheets and a tiger print blanket strewn across it. A disco ball hangs at the center of the room that blinks in blue and purple lights.

And just as you notice handcuffs at the foot of the bed, you run upstairs and out the front door, thanking Abby and her gang of misfits for their concert.

You keep everything you and your friends do to yourself since social media doesn't exist. Of course, if you filmed your weekly antics, you would most likely be TikTok famous, but the beauty in your innocent adventures is that only you experience them.

Life will continue to get better and funnier from here. You, Sarah, and Carter will create hysterical memories for yourselves, and you'll learn to genuinely love who you are because of how much they adore you.

Your heart will open to new love again. You'll feel the same as you did in your last relationship, but better. More accepted, seen, and understood. And lucky for you, you can't get mono twice.

Just remember that you're doing the best you can, and your best is exactly where you're supposed to be.

I love you, and you're perfect.

Love,
DANIELLE

Silent Suffering

Dear Danielle,

You're in your first year of college!

...And you're not so sure if you like it.

Your friends who are away at other schools tell you about their wild weekends of partying, and all you can account for is witnessing a spontaneous drum circle with barefoot students in the quad outside your dorm.

Oh, and there was a party from a student in the acting conservatory, but he wouldn't let you in his apartment because if you're not in acting classes, you're not welcome. You wonder if Purchase College is just an extension of high school.

You make friends with the girls across the hall from you and thank God for them because they're your saving grace throughout the two years you stay at Purchase. Your weekends of partying consist of getting drunk in your dorm room and summoning your inner child to play pranks on people again.

You and your friend Aria are so bored one Friday night that you top off a bottle of Smirnoff and post fake flyers around the school notifying everyone of a: "MISSING MUSTACHE! PLEASE CALL IF YOU SEE IT!" You list your friend's number and include a photo of him with a photoshopped mustache as the contact information for any queries. You'll laugh at this for many years to come.

You know this isn't the college experience you dreamed of, but you make the best of it and love being away from home. Meeting new people is refreshing. You're an optimistic person who tries to find the good in everything. Some people say this mindset dwindles as time transpires, but your positivity doesn't waver as you get older. You still choose to highlight a person's strengths instead of their weaknesses. You still know how to turn a negative circumstance into a learning experience. You still try your hardest to love yourself even when the cards are stacked against you.

In your sophomore year as an undergrad, your boyfriend applies to Purchase and is accepted into the photography conservatory. You're both elated to spend more time together since you've been doing long distance for the last year. Even though you missed him every hour of the day, you loved visiting Las Vegas and doing impromptu photo shoots in the desert. You adore how he's the first person to show you the type of relationship you always dreamed of but never had. You pinch yourself because you can't believe you have found the perfect guy.

Your first three weeks of being on campus together are a dream come true. You eat waffles in the quad, hold hands while walking to class, take the bus into town to get grilled cheeses at the local diner, and collaborate on creative projects at night. Everything lines up exactly the way you envisioned it.

Until it doesn't anymore.

Nick makes new friends in his classes and begins breaking plans with you to hang out with them. He stays up past midnight editing photos in the darkroom of the photography building with female students from his class. He takes pictures of girls in the dancing conservatory for their audition photos. He smokes two to three times a day with his roommates and their girlfriends outside their dorm. And you notice in the limited moments when you're together how he seems to know 90% of the female body at Purchase.

Your stomach is in knots every hour of the day. You can barely pay attention in class. You lose five pounds from excessive worrying. You ask your friends for advice that you never take. And you wish Nick never encroached on your college experience.

You wish he were still across the country when he liked calling you at random hours of the day just to hear your voice. You wish he'd morph back into the boyfriend who couldn't get enough of you.

Where did that guy go?

Whenever you confront him about his behavior and lack of interest in you or your relationship, he makes you feel crazy. He swears up and down that he isn't doing anything wrong and just enjoys making new friends. When you ask him why you're never invited to hang out with them, he tells you that he didn't think he needed to extend an invitation.

You're always free to hang out with us, babe.

So, you decide one Friday night to drop by his friend's party, unannounced and technically uninvited, even though the unspoken code is that you're always welcome. Once you open the door to the two-story complex, you immediately sense that something's off. Your heart pounds in a panic. You know in your gut that you'll soon set eyes on what you were hoping wasn't true.

As you wave smoke from your eyes and wipe sweat from your forehead, you walk upstairs and make your way toward the den. Nick's on the couch with a joint in his hand in the corner of the room, and a girl you recognize is sitting on his lap, laughing and whispering into his ear. She takes a hit from his joint and grabs his head, turning his lips toward hers, and exhales into his mouth. He stares up at her in infatuation — a slightly heightened version of how he used to look at you. You feel like you're going to throw up or faint.

When he sees you watching, you turn around to escape the party as fast as you can. You cry as you push drunk teenagers out of the way to step outside and get fresh air. You feel like you can't breathe. You feel like you can't see. Everything around you is crumbling.

Just as your face hits the cold, fall air, Nick's hands are on yours as he tries to pull you toward him. He yells and begs for you to listen. He wasn't doing anything wrong. Gina is just a good friend, and they like smoking together. She's wasted, and so is he, and he got caught up in the moment and realizes how bad it looks, and if you could just take a walk with him and listen, he'll prove to you that he didn't mess up. He never experienced college before. He still loves you.

You don't want to hear it, but you do. You don't want to walk away, but you do. You don't want to cry all night over someone who clearly doesn't care about you, but you do. You don't want to break up with him, but you do.

The following week is one of the hardest of your life, but you have a trip to New Orleans planned with Purchase students to rebuild houses after Hurricane Katrina. The last thing you want is to get on a plane when you're devastated, raw, and heartbroken but you pull yourself together because getting away is better than staying in New York.

This ends up being the best thing for you. You meet amazing people who feel like lifelong friends. They help you get through your heartache. They encourage you to see what you deserve in a boyfriend. They inspire you to stand your ground and remain single.

When you get home, the impressions from your trip fasten to your heart for as long as they can, until day by day, they fade. Your resistance weakens with every call and text from

Nick. You don't want to be alone. You don't want to be sad. You don't want to continue moping through your life.

Maybe if you weren't together at Purchase, you'd return to the couple you used to be. Maybe if he could see the kind of girlfriend you always were, he'd realize what he had. Maybe if you started fresh somewhere new, you could give him a second chance.

I wish I could go back and step into your shoes to stop you from doing what you're about to do, but I know everything has its purpose. Every person and experience in your life is there for a reason.

You're learning through torment and silent suffering how to love yourself. Sometimes that's only learned from being shown how you don't want to be loved.

I love you. You're perfect. You're still doing the best you can, and your best is just right.

Love,
DANIELLE

COMING HOME

Dear Danielle,

You're living in Las Vegas and work as a barista at the Starbucks a few blocks away from Nick's parents' home. You love being thousands of miles away from New York. You can reinvent yourself to be whoever you want to be. This sense of freedom is addicting, and you claim that you'll never return to Long Island. You can't imagine how you lived there before.

You and Nick spend your weekends partying across the street at the ex-porn star's house; she throws extravagant blowouts that last until six in the morning. You love meeting offbeat and eccentric people, and imagine that if your life were a movie, you'd be Kate Hudson in *Almost Famous*. You're wild, spontaneous, and chase after a good time.

Love in Las Vegas is what you'd expect it to be for two twenty-year-olds. You're in love one minute and tearing at each other's throats the next. You find an email in his inbox from Gina. She said she misses him and wishes he was in her bed.

He's still lying to you. Something he swears he'll stop doing time and time again.

You force yourself to believe it's real love when he tries to convince you of his commitment by grabbing your arms so hard they bruise for days later. Or when he gets infuriated while driving to Hollywood Video that he slams his foot on the gas and spins the steering wheel until the car spirals out of control and heads toward a streetlight. By the grace of invisible forces or fate, you miss slamming into the stiff metal pole by a sliver of a second. Or when he stampedes into your bedroom and steals your book from your hands to rip it into pieces and take into the backyard to set it on fire. He sits watching it burn until there's nothing left of it.

What you think will be the last of his outbursts ends up piling over into a series of incidents that can no longer be counted on two hands. Your body begins to tell a story and without you having to say a word, you decide to give him one last chance. One last time. You'll leave for good if he acts out again…right?

When he resents you for expecting more than what he can give you, you start spending time with the Starbucks crew. At this point, Nick has stopped including you in his weekly plans, so you create a life without him, even though you return to the same home at the end of the day. You try to prove to yourself and your family that you don't need your old life in New York. Things will be okay. They always are. This is just another bump in the road that you and Nick will crawl out of. You've gotten used to traveling on hands and knees to make it through each week. This will be no different.

Flash forward to the following month, and Nick isn't the only liar in your relationship anymore. When he flies to Long Island to visit a friend one weekend (a friend you later find out is Gina), you go to a house party with the baristas. You catch Kara's roommate, Tyler, staring at you throughout most of the night, and you blush at the attention. Nick hasn't looked at you in that way for months.

You step outside to pour yourself a beer from the keg to find Tyler standing next to it with the nozzle in his hand. You talk for what feels like an eternity, and when you go for a walk to escape the noise of the party, he leans in to kiss you, and you don't flinch. It surprises you how much you enjoy kissing someone else.

What have you been holding onto that's prevented you from feeling appreciated, seen, and desired? When's the last time you were truly happy?

When you wake up the next day, you don't regret kissing Tyler, but you wish you didn't tell him about the consequences of Nick's anger. You're embarrassed to admit what you never thought your life would become. But, when he told you that he's just a phone call away and will drop whatever he's doing if you needed him, your heart mellowed, and a wall dropped. The protection of a stranger offered more security in a single night than you've felt with Nick for years.

You spend your first summer as a twenty-one-year-old backpacking throughout Italy with your cousin, Katie, and Sarah, and realize that the freedom you once felt in Vegas is only a fraction of what you experience in Europe. You fall in love with everything. The pizza, wine, rolling oceans, cobblestone roads, the laidback nature of Italians, the magnificent view from balconies in Positano, the language and love present in everything around you.

Your life is forever changed by what you see in your travels, and you promise yourself that you'll remember the feeling of unbridled infatuation and appreciation for life.

When you come home, this awakening frees you from Nick for good. Italy taught you how to be brave and bold and to expect only the best for yourself.

You learn self-love again and realize how much happier you can be alone than with someone else. Instead of playing it small with small people, you promise yourself that your next love will be big and courageous.

You're learning and growing so much. I love you.

Love,
DANIELLE

WILD RESILIENCE

Dear Danielle,

It's 3 a.m. on a Tuesday in December. You just woke up, and there's no one sleeping beside you. You check your phone, and there are no missed calls or texts. You get up and look out the living room window. There's no one outside.

He did it again. He promised he wouldn't, but you're realizing his promises hold no weight lately.

You call him, no response.

You call again, no answer.

Shocker.

The third time you call, he picks up. He's at a club or bar—there's loud music and women's laughter in the background.

Heyyyy babe, what's up? Are you here?

No, I'm home. Where are you?

In the city with clients! Hold on...I'll be there in one sec! Save me a shot!

You told me you'd have dinner and a drink instead of coming home black-out. You promised me you'd stop doing this.

Babe, stop. Come on. It's just wooorkkk. Don't be mad. I had to take my clients out!

You hang up and take a deep breath as the tears arrive at

their normal hour. You don't know what to do. You love him, but you don't love how he makes you feel. You're jealous, insecure, and untrusting around him. You worry that he's cheating. From the looks of it, he is. But you don't know for sure. You never do.

Even when you snoop through his phone after he comes home from a night of drinking, you can never find anything concrete enough to leave. There's always just enough to make you suspicious but nothing evidential to solve your case. If you disclose your findings to him, you become the crazy, uptight girlfriend who must learn to trust him. He always has an alibi for whatever you discover. You almost wish you'd stumble upon a clandestine text, photo, or voicemail to trigger you to do what you know you need to.

You're terrified of moving out of your apartment and returning home to mom and dad. You're almost thirty. You don't want to live out of your old childhood bedroom again until you find your own place. Even though you sometimes look around the walls of your home and wonder when you'll move out on your own, you still try to preserve whatever's left of your relationship.

You don't want to call your friends and vent because you know the advice they will give you. Advice you never take. They don't want to hear it anymore. How many times can you complain about his benders and never do anything about it? You're too scared to take action. You've been together for four years. You're not sure how you just give that up.

So, as you've grown accustomed to for most of your life, you stay. You settle. You play make-believe and hope this time he sticks to his word. All you have to do is threaten to leave for good with a little more sternness to your voice. Don't let him see that you're dying inside. Play it cool and pretend that if you had to leave, you'd be fine on your own.

He'll be so scared that you're serious he wouldn't dare do anything to fuck it up again.

He swears on everything he owns that he'll stop drinking.

It's 2 a.m. on a Saturday in March. Your hands reach for the pillow next to you, and there's a cold, empty space. Like clockwork, your heart drops into your stomach, and adrenaline pumps through your veins. You grab your phone from the nightstand. No missed calls. No new texts.

You're not calling him.

But what if he's hurt? What if something happened? What if he's in the hospital? What if he's dead?

No. You won't engage these questions that love to interrogate you in the wake of his absence. You know he's okay. He's probably still awake and partying somewhere as you lay here alone and try coaxing yourself to sleep.

Don't you dare call. He doesn't deserve to hear from you.

3 a.m. arrives, and no update.

4 a.m. rolls in with a deafening silence.

5, 6, 7, 8 a.m. …nothing.

You get up and throw on jeans and a black shirt for your bartending shift. When afternoon arrives, and you've still heard no word, you begin to panic.

What if something did happen?

You call his friend who he was with last night.

He never came home? Really? I left the city around 11 p.m. He was still hanging out when I left. Now you have me worried…

You receive a call at 1 p.m.

He's okay. He just drank a little too much and passed out at a friend's apartment. He's sorry. He knows how it looks, but it's not what you think. Please don't do anything extreme. He'll be home soon and can explain everything.

Danielle, I know how hard this moment is for you and how difficult the next few months will be, but this will be the last time you cry in the bathroom at work over him. This will be the last time you seek approval from your coworkers and regulars for staying with him. This will be the last time you have to force yourself into silencing your intuition for him.

This, Danielle, is what sets you free.

Not just from him or your pattern of settling, but from believing that you deserve anything less than what your heart desires.

When you pack your belongings and move out, there's an impenetrable force guiding you that you've never felt before. There's a strong and fierce woman leading the way.

I know you've never felt more scared, but I promise you that everything will be okay. You are going to be okay.

Because what happens when you listen to yourself and face your fears is that divine intervention enters your life. Magic walks through the front door. And even though you can't see it yet, the life you've been dreaming of is emerging. You're rising into who you were always destined to be.

You're about to embark on your life's grandest adventure. You're about to fall in love with who you are for the first time in your life.

I can't wait for you to experience it. I'll meet you there.

Sending you love and encouragement from just a stone's throw away.

I love you.

Love,
DANIELLE

THIS IS YOUR TIME
NOW

Dear Danielle,

You just made the scariest decision of your life. You left everything that was comfortable and secure for a world filled with darkness. But don't worry, it won't be that way for long. You'll find your way again.

The thing about people, experiences, and situations that feel comfortable for us but no longer allow us to grow is that they don't offer the security we genuinely desire. There's more security in the unknown and uncharted if only we believed in its ability to catch us when we finally take the leap.

You jumped with arms wide open, eyes looking toward the horizon, and didn't dare look for what was beneath you. I'm so proud of you for choosing yourself, Danielle. I'm so proud of the woman you're becoming by loving yourself first.

It's been a long journey for you to get to this place, but can you see how important that journey was? How every single step you took led you to where you are now? Without those steps, you wouldn't possess the bravery and courage to set your whole world on fire and watch it burn around you.

You are going to get through this, I promise.

I know you can't see it yet. I know everything feels cold and lonely, but there's a light ahead, waiting for you to greet it. There's a soft opening reaching out its hand for you to hold. There's adventure there, beyond the peak. It's what you've been dreaming of.

Without taking this risk, you'd never find what you're looking for.

Without letting go of what's no longer meant for you, you'd never discover yourself.

Without choosing darkness for some time, you'd never step into the light.

This is your time now, Danielle.

This is where it all begins for you.

I love you.

Love,
DANIELLE

A LETTER TO FEAR

To my Beloved Fear,

How are you?

Are you still hiding in the shadows of my mind? Are you still lurking within the chambers of my heart?

My love, I hear you. I see you. I love you.

You don't need to step forward the moment I desire change. There's no reason to rush toward center stage when I realize that I'm ready for something more.

I understand that you want to protect me. You believe that by holding me still in what has always been, you're keeping me safe. But haven't we learned by now that we don't grow in familiar spaces? Aren't we living proof that change is the only constant in life? Haven't we learned that to deny change is to disregard the very nature of our beings? The very essence of life?

I know I'm destined for grand and beautiful things. I know that it will require hard work to get to where I want to be, but I'm willing and ready to become who I am. For, in essence, I already am that which I desire to be.

Please stop visiting me and telling me that I don't have what it takes to live my dream. Please stop putting me down the moment I make a mistake. Please stop encouraging me to compare myself to others when I believe I should be twenty steps ahead of where I am.

Can't you see? I've already grown so much from where I used to be. I want to be grateful for where I am. I want to love who I am. I don't want to disregard my process.

When you're present, I worry that things will never change and that I'll forever be on a loop of the same cycles, patterns, and habits that aren't serving me.

I love you for your efforts to protect me, but I don't need you right now, and I lovingly set you free. Please know that I'll always be okay, and I'll always be here for you, just as you are there for me. But for now, we can part ways. I'm okay on my own.

I trust that we'll find each other again, and when we do, we'll work together to create beauty rather than mistrust, love rather than pain, and peace rather than chaos.

My beloved fear, I love you. I thank you. I honor you.

Love,
DANIELLE

A NEW VOICE

Dear Danielle,

You're learning to quiet the outside voices and listen more intently to your own.

You're alone, but not lonely.

You're struggling, but at peace.

You're fulfilled, but still longing.

You're always going to be a bundle of paradoxes. You're always going to wish you were one or the other. You're always going to be hungry with feverous desires. And you're learning to be okay with that.

You're learning to love yourself.

There wasn't any choice but to love yourself when living alone in quarantine. It was just you and your writing, and you enjoyed every last drop of solitude. You've become quite the hermit, though when you retreat indoors, you travel to other worlds through your creativity. You now spend some of the most fulfilling times of your life alone. Isolation from the outside world has stirred a love affair of self in you.

Isn't it funny how you used to cling to people and relationships for security, and now the only assurance you rely on is your own resilience?

I couldn't be prouder of who you are right now. You're becoming the vision of yourself that you always desired, and that's entirely a result of your own doing—no one else's. Stop for a moment and honor how far you've come. You need to value your growth as you're growing and not only when you've blossomed.

I know it's difficult to focus on all the positives in your life when there's so much change happening. Quarantine and Covid brought both blessings and rude awakenings.

The year 2020 offered you the time and space to focus on your writing and embrace the present moment. You practiced mindfulness by taking small bites of your food and savoring the taste of your meals. When you read a book, you didn't pick up your phone for distractions; you delighted in each word. When you needed a break, you let yourself relax. When the sun was setting, and your carpet had large patches of sunlight stretched across it, you laid down and lingered in its warmth. You dozed off for hours. You laughed at funny movies and cried during sad ones. You spent hours on Zoom with family and friends. You took long walks alone. You practiced yoga and meditation. You praised the little things.

2021 provided a different kind of awakening.

You learned that life could change and throw your world off its axis at any given time. No one is exempt from getting cancer. You aren't immortal. Friends you thought would remain by your side can abandon you when you need them the most. Authenticity in those closest to you can fade into superficiality as you grow older. And even when you're afraid to speak your truth and stand up for what you believe in, you should always share your voice. The worst that can happen is you get trolled on the internet. The best that can happen is you see people for who they are.

What you're going through is forcing you to look at your life differently. Who are you, and who do you want to be? What have you been doing that isn't serving you, and what can you do to raise your vibration? What type of people do you want to surround yourself with? How do you want to spend your time? When will you start living the life that you always dreamed of?

The interesting thing about dark nights of the soul and hard seasons is that they strip you until you're left with nothing, and it's only until you have nothing that you can see the truth in its most vulnerable form. It's not easy viewing the comforts that once made you feel safe in their naked essence. Once the veil is lifted, there's no going back to what used to be. You can't unsee the truth.

You experience a thousand mini deaths in a single revelation. You also experience a thousand rebirths. That's how each day feels lately. You rise and fall as you try to ground yourself in what no longer is and what you're trying to make your life become. It's because of how much you're hurting that you're growing as fast and immensely as you are.

I know you want to call your friends and have things be the way they always were when you'd laugh on the phone for hours over nonsensical absurdities. But you're angry for being judged for your views on sensitive topics the world just recently had the opportunity to form an opinion on. You're resentful that they excluded you from birthday and holiday plans because you had the bravery to publicly share your voice when they disagreed with you. You're upset that a friendship as long and dependable as yours even got to this point. And you're worried that you may never reclaim what you've lost, even though you're not entirely sure you want it back.

I know you wish Bailey was still here so you could talk to him about this and then make prank phone calls in your apartment to laugh your worries away. I know how hard it is to fully grasp the weight of him being gone forever. I know how rare it is for you to find people you connect with on a deeper level and who see you for who you are, which makes his passing even more painful. Give yourself patience and love right now because you've never lost someone so close to you before and healing takes time. It's okay for you to take your time.

I know you worry about your sister and her health. Watching her endure chemotherapy and witnessing the aftermath of such a strong treatment was one of the most onerous burdens you've ever had to carry. You admire your sister's fortitude and resilience, and whenever you fear receiving a similar diagnosis, you remember how strong she is. Even when she was at her worst, when she couldn't get out of bed and discovered hair all over her apartment, she still wore a face of bravery. Even though she felt broken and is still learning how to pick up the pieces to reshape her life, your family formed an indestructible bond that strengthened your love. You're so incredibly lucky to have the family that you do.

Through all the unexpected changes you've weathered, you've found that your sisters, parents, cousins, and a few close friends are your support system and can help you get through anything. There are people in your life that will be there for you no matter what. They accept you as you are. They love you as you are. *They* are your people.

As you move forward into this new year, take comfort in knowing that you survived the most taxing year of your life. You not only survived, but you also rose above every hurdle you once thought you'd never be able to overcome. Take that energy of perseverance and let it lead your life. The more challenges you endure, the more you expand your comfort zones. The more uncomfortable you get, the more confident you become when you conquer your fears.

How many more fears can you defeat?

This is the year you make your dreams come true, Danielle.

This is your time to show the world everything you have to offer.

This is the path that will lead you home.

I love you.

Love,
DANIELLE

WRITING YOURSELF A LETTER

If you want to try writing yourself a letter, I suggest creating a quiet and relaxing space for yourself. Grab your journal and begin writing your greeting. You can use your real name, nickname, or any other title you call yourself. Whenever I do this with my high school creative writing students, I always enjoy reading their greetings. I've seen, "Yo, kid!" "What's Up, Royalty," "Hi There, Beautiful Girl," or "Sup, Sucka!"

What I love most about assigning letters to my students is how honest they are with themselves. They address their faults and mistakes head-on. They know what they need to work on. They try to be encouraging even if they don't feel encouraged themselves. And they're specific on what they're currently going through so they can better understand themselves. They also want to ensure they write a good letter to their future selves since I mail it back to them a year later.

To me, this assignment isn't about having perfect grammar, structure, or syntax. Instead, it's about tapping into your emotions and life experiences to create a more trusting relationship with yourself. It's about loving who you are through your ups and downs, highs and lows, mistakes and successes. It's about being true to yourself at any point in life and remembering that at the end of the day, you're your own best friend.

So, pick up your journal, get cozy, light your favorite

candle, play soothing music, grab a snug blanket, and write.

Write to your past, present, or future self from who you are today. Write a letter to your present or future self from your past self. Write a letter to your past or present self from your future self. Let the words flow. Don't judge what comes onto the page. Don't worry if it's not poetic or if it even makes sense.

Take a deep breath, choose a time in your life that you'd like to work on and heal, and simply move your pen by trusting your voice and listening to your heart.

It can be as simple as that if you allow it to be.

Loving and supporting yourself can be as easy as you make it.

CHAPTER 7
LETTERS TO THE MEN
I LOVED

Dear Reader,

Have you ever had a hard time letting something or someone go? Have you ever felt like it takes you longer to heal from wounds than most people? Have you ever had words left unsaid that you needed to say, in some shape or form, so they'd no longer be locked inside—even if you were the only one hearing them?

Some of the deepest wounds I've experienced were from heartbreak. Losing someone who was once present in my everyday world, a person who was an integral part of my daily routine, caused both physical and emotional pain. In the same way I've learned to cope with personal upset by writing letters to myself, I have written letters to past loves.

If I felt wronged, misunderstood, hurt, or angry, I'd begin writing the words I needed to say. When I was done writing, I'd realize that the only person who needed to hear those words were me. I never ended up sending them.

The letters, poems, and prose in this chapter are some of my favorite pieces I've written. They were born from the deepest pain I've experienced, and they remind me that even when it feels impossible to carry on, heartbreak has always given me gifts I never knew I needed.

I hope you find the gifts, lessons, and raw, impenetrable beauty in your heartbreak, too.

Sending love always,
DANIELLE

I MISS, I WISH...YOU WELL

I woke up missing you this morning. I miss the way you'd stare, your eyes like lungs, breathing me in.

I miss your hands, how you always knew where to place them. When to move the tips of your fingers along the curve of my back, and when to settle your palms on mine.

I miss your sweetness, your genuine desire to make me happy. I wish I recognized that more then. I wish I realized how I'd never met someone like you before. How I'd never been treated with such respect, admiration, and care.

I miss the person I was when standing alongside you: kinder, less judgmental, willing to see the light under shadows, and always rare in your gaze.

What I miss the most about you are things I never realized I wanted or needed in love, but are now tiny cracks waiting to be filled.

What I'm saying is that I wish I had missed you before.

I wish I appreciated all that you offered so generously, patiently, and quietly for so long.

What I'm trying to say is that you're as extraordinary as you made me believe I was, and you deserve someone—a love—as special as you are.

I'm sorry that person wasn't me, but I know you'll find her.

And when you do, if she makes you feel a fraction of how you loved me, then you'll be home.

IF ONLY WE COULD
GO BACK

I remember you looking at me from across a candlelit table as though I was the most beautiful woman you'd ever seen. Your eyes were radiant when you listened to me speak about my dreams.

I remember long dinners with personal exchanges — the kind of conversation that opens buried memories, unspoken longings, and fears not yet recognized. You told me you'd never spoken to someone so candidly before, and I felt rare for being the person you were yourself with.

I remember nights undressing before you, your hands on my face, then running through the dusk of my hair, slowly unzipping garments dropped to the floor, and I'd feel both whole and vulnerable, eager for you to show me how you love in the dark.

I remember the first time you said you loved me. We were in the city, and you didn't mean to blurt it so suddenly. But, when you did, your cheeks blushed, and nervous laughter filled the silence until I told you I loved you too.

I remember long drives where you'd grab my hand, look over, and smile. You'd sing the lyrics to a new band you were excited about, and I'd listen as I was filled with a warmth I'd never known before.

I can't remember when the thread between us started thinning, when we stopped noticing each other. I can't recall the exact moment when our light began to dim.

I wish I knew what caused a love like ours to burn and exhaust itself.

Sometimes I wonder if I could just go back to the day, the hour, or minute that we didn't recognize ourselves in each other anymore—if only I could make you see me the way you did during our first night together—then maybe our story would be different.

What do you do when a journey hasn't reached its peak? What happens when your mind is stuck in the past? What would you say if I were to return to you with arms open, eyes lambent and alive, ready to try again?

Would you feel the same if I told you that most days, I dream of a love that comes close to ours but worry I may never find it?

If only we could return to the nights when we saw each other in a crowded room. If only we could remember what kept us close. If only you could see yourself in me again.

If only.

DREAMS

I had a dream about you again last night. I was floating down a river, my arms outstretched, hair swaying with the ease of the current, and my eyes set on the clouds above me. The sun was soon to be replaced by the moon, and as I drifted toward land, I saw you sitting by the water's edge. You looked up and spotted me with eager eyes. As we waded toward each other, the current accelerated, and I couldn't swim against it.

I tried to reach for you, desperate for my fingers to meet yours, but the river was moving too fast, and I was seized in the rush downstream. As I drifted further, all I saw was you standing against the rocky landscape on the bank, paralyzed and unable to help me.

I don't know why whenever I dream about you, it's as though we're two worlds apart, always lingering away, just when we're about to be together.

Sometimes before I sleep, I ask that our hands touch, our arms lock around each other, and our lungs breathe the same air. But every night when I close my eyes, you're either miles away or directly in front of me, and still, I can never hold you.

It's funny; I'm beginning to wonder if I ever had you when we were together. If you were ever truly mine.

When the constellations tell their stories tonight, I'll make a different request. If I must dream of you, I'll ask that I don't see you, even if you're in the distance or nearby. That you don't call for me.

I don't know how many nights I've spent searching for

your eyes like a lighthouse in a misty sky, waiting for you to lead me home.

But you're no longer home, and I think it's time that I let you go.

Dream Analysis

Have you ever woken up from a dream that felt so real you couldn't stop thinking about it? I always find those dreams to be the most unsettling when they're about an ex-boyfriend or girlfriend because they stir old emotions and tenderize your heart. It's like walking around with exposed wounds on your skin. As strange as this experience can be, this type of energy is best for a good writing session. It's easier to access your emotions when you're vulnerable and sensitive.

When is the last time you had a dream that made you feel off the following day? Can you write about that dream in as much detail as you can remember? Where were you, and who were you with? What does the location of your dream and the people in it symbolize for you? How do they make you feel? How were you feeling in the dream? What other objects and sensations can you remember? What do those objects and sensations represent to you, and what emotions do they produce? What lessons do you think they were trying to teach you?

The more of a response you can give for each question, the better idea you'll have of why you had this specific dream. Dreams are a form of communication from our subconscious mind to our waking mind. The way to analyze a dream and uncover its meaning is by dissecting each detail to divulge what significance it holds for you. It's easy to do a Google search for dream symbolism, but the best way to understand your dream is to make it unique for *you*.

When you analyze your dreams in this way, you'll understand yourself better. So, instead of walking around feeling heavy from an unexpected dream, you can move through the day with a heightened awareness of the inner workings of your heart and mind.

DWELL A MOMENT LONGER

I have moments where missing you overwhelms me. It comes like heavy rainfall on a clear morning. Like cold water hitting bare skin after a warm bath. Like bringing my hand too close to a flame.

Missing you is sharp and unwavering. Like a phantom pain in my limbs, my body aches and longs for you as though you're an essential part of its makeup. As though you belong within me somewhere, like you once did.

I never know what to expect or how to brace for it. I only know that when you arrive, I let you overpower me. If I allow you to consume me, then maybe I can feel you for a moment longer.

Lately, you visit me in the early morning hours, between the soothed and subdued sky. I see you in the slow and steady movement of the trees outside my window. I hear you in the stir and rustle of the bushes in the wind. I feel you as though you're standing behind me, arms wrapped around my shoulders, your face buried in the arch of my neck.

You shake me from my waking life, and suddenly I'm taken back to the day we met and how I was drawn to you like a magnetic force I had no control in resisting. Even now, I have no control.

Would you think I was crazy if I told you that I like the discomfort of missing you? That I wait for it to visit me because then I feel connected to something?

Do you miss me too, or have you already erased our history?

To me, you're still a storyboard with photos, quotes, and mementos threaded together by a string.

I hope my face is still in your memory, that I haven't become an empty canvas waiting to be filled with memories from another. Please tell me that you haven't disregarded me, that I still hold some space in the back of your mind. If not in your mind, allow me to dwell a moment longer in your heart.

Maybe I'm a phantom pain you experience from time to time, too. Maybe we're both just waking and dreaming, somehow still caught between the day we first set eyes on each other and the night we said goodbye.

BE AS YOU ARE

Sit with yourself. Sit with your loneliness. Sit with the sensation of missing someone. Take a deep breath. Exhale long and slowly. Let the tears fall. Let yourself be as you are.

I Don't Want to Forget You

I wonder when I'll stop thinking about you.
When will I remember you as you were,
instead of how I'm imagining you to be?
I'm afraid that I don't want to forget you.
I don't want to lose our memories,
even if they were overshadowed
toward the end.

I came home lonely last night.
I slept with someone else's body.
His mouth covered mine.
I laid on his bed
and as his tongue traveled
over me,
I tried to feel complete.
I wanted to make
what we were doing
enough.
I hoped he was
all I've been waiting for.

But once I closed my door,
I dropped
to the floor,
and my heart ached for you.

This longing that comes over me

in the middle of the night,
this static space where I need you
is a stinging sadness
I don't know how to quit.

I return to you
when I can't find
what I'm looking for.
When another person
leaves me empty,
my thoughts run to you
to fill me up.

But I'm never full.
I never was.

I keep trying to find someone
to see me the way I desire to be seen,
and I'm realizing
that I've never been seen.

Not by you
or him.
Only by me.

And I'm worrying
if I haven't found it yet,
will I ever?

Will I ever mend the throbbing tenderness
tearing open my chest?
Will I ever stop returning to you?

Why are you still my home
when you abandoned me?

How will I ever discover home
in another man

when I continue looking for you
in them?

THIS TIME I'M STANDING

Every time you step back
into my life
you leave me lonely.

It doesn't take much;
a phone call,
a message with your name on it,
your voice,
the scent of your collarbone,
the strand of hair that stands
higher than the others
at the tip of your forehead,
the way you know me
better than anyone else.

Sometimes I want to travel
back to us.
Sometimes I'm tempted
to tread our familiar waters;
to be held by someone
so warmly and comfortably,
without anything needing to be said.
Without anything needing to be heard.

Sometimes I wish
I didn't think
as intricately and meticulously

as I do.
Then maybe I could
enjoy momentary bliss.

The dents that I filled
from your absence
grow deeper
each time we speak.

It doesn't matter
how long it's been,
how much I've grown,
how confident I am,
or solid I feel,
just your presence
digs holes in me.

I'm beginning to think
you like to dig.

You like me raw,
messy,
unbridled.

You enjoy seeing me hurt.
If I hurt, then I still love you,
and if I still love you,
then maybe there's a chance
for us again.

But I can't keep bleeding
from wounds
that will never fully heal.

I can't continue returning
to what was.

As much as I'd love
to crawl back to you

on hands and knees,
to be picked up
and loved
and seen,
I've already been there,
on the floor,
waiting for you.

I've already waited too long.

This time I'm standing.

This time I'm choosing me.

THE PHANTOM IN
MY SLEEP

Dear Nick,

It feels funny writing you a letter; it's been so long now. How many years is it? Seven or eight? Time gets blurry when we have so many beginnings, endings, and in-betweens.

I still think about you from time to time. Your face paves its way into a random weeknight dream, and somehow, I wake up not feeling like myself. I wonder if it will always be that way with you. If ten years down the road, you'll still slither into the driftless stirrings of my life. If you'll peek your head in to compare the way things were then to how they are with someone new.

All you did was hurt me; I don't know why I still think of you. It's not intentional. I'm not missing you or us, but sometimes I catch glimpses of how your dark eyes met mine and how you had this perplexity I never fully understood. As much as I knew you, I didn't know you. There was always another layer to unravel, a new personality to learn.

How is it that someone reckless beyond measure is still hiding in the alleys of my mind? What is it about you that I can't rid myself of?

I've met many others after you. Men who were kinder, stronger, more stable, and more responsive. Men that far surpassed who you'll ever become. But it was your subtlety that was the most intriguing and your mystery that pulls me back in when it wants to.

Do you still think of it, too?

Do you remember how it felt in the beginning? When your hands crossed mine, our bodies pressed together, and how we were the only two in any room?

I do. And I remember what it was like to leave you.

The mourning that was subsided by my liberty. The freedom that rose when I was finally immune to you.

But maybe you're something dormant—passive and inert until triggered.

What triggers you, Nick? What evokes the sensation of my lips on yours? What inches you toward regret?

You used to be my trigger. You knew how to call forth beauty. You were skillful at enraging pain.

You're a memory that's fading. A light that's gone dim. A phantom that only comes to life when I'm sleeping.

Love,
DANIELLE

I Always Wanted to
Be Seen

Dear Mason,

When I look back at our history, I feel like I'm watching a foreign film without subtitles. You're as transient to me now as a stranger would be, and the truth is I felt glimpses of that when we were together, too.

You were obsessed with the image of who you tried to be—a man emotionless and authoritative. It petrified you to unearth who you truly are. I couldn't wait any longer for you to become the version of yourself I always hoped you'd be. It wasn't my job to break down your walls to unleash your vulnerability. You had to learn how to do that yourself.

Leaving was easy. I always imagined that our eventual split would take me a while to get over. I dreaded it but knew it was inevitable. We'd be sharing dinner at our favorite Italian restaurant, traipsing the lower east side of Manhattan, embarking on excursions in a new country, and any time I'd open up to you, you never had an authentic reply. Everything was one-word answers, a go-to script of acceptable responses. Nothing came from the depths of you. Is there a depth to you?

I was desperate to be seen by you, but you didn't have the ability to see me, and I understand now that it wasn't your fault. What I tried to pull from you, you never had to begin with. It was my fault for getting frustrated that you weren't who I wanted you to be. It was my fault that I stayed as long as I did.

I wish I could say that I remember good times together, but the girl who I was with you compared to who I am now doesn't believe in the same version of happiness. Contentment to me then was a dulled complacency. A second voice questioned what I thought was my serenity. I was so accustomed to interrogating myself that it became my normal.

If you were to ask me years ago if I was happy, I'd probably say yes. We had special moments together, memories that are exclusive to us, but after I left, I expanded my idea of what I wanted to feel and experience. If I learned anything from you, it's that I desire something rich and all-consuming. As with anything in my life, I don't want to play small.

And you, Mason, thought the way you were living was playing large, but I know you felt so small. I wonder if you still do.

I hope you don't.

Love,
DANIELLE

WE ARE UNTETHERED
FROM DARKNESS

Dear Marco,

How are you? Your photos pop up on my laptop from time to time. You seem like you're doing well. Life in Europe looks so alluring.

The rolling curves of the Amalfi Coast; the crystal water cascading from ocean waves; guitarists on street corners playing for themselves and the night sky; the romance that's blooming within every crevice of its landscape. It's easy to fall in love when there's boundless love around you.

I remember how every experience with you was magnified by the beauty of our scenery and the new terrain I had yet to discover.

I never felt so liberated. Life in Italy was unrestrained. I would walk the cobblestone streets, gaze out to the golden hues flowering the cliffside, and feel a warmth surround me, as though everything happening in that moment was meant for me.

Days stretched into weeks, and before I knew it, I was waiting at the airport to return home. I didn't know how I could love New York as much as I loved Positano. Life had never been so gratifying before my month-long stay in Italy. I brimmed with happiness. I was drenched in bliss.

I didn't know where my leaving left us, but I thought we

both understood the nature of what we were. We had more than just an ocean between us. We were at two completely different points in our lives.

I'm sorry that I assumed you felt the same way as me. I never meant to hurt you. I know you were willing to come to New York, to leave one life and start another, but I wasn't ready for that. I didn't want to be responsible for you moving your life for me.

And looking back now, I know my decision was right. I don't know if you see it that way, too, but I hope you do.

Some things are better left when they're at their best. We don't always have to wait for their eventual fall. Our memory is untethered to heartache or pain. We're untouched by darkness, forever preserved in the goodness of our sweet beginning.

Love,
DANIELLE

THE REARVIEW
MIRROR

Dear Finn,

I met you while I was bartending. Coming right off a breakup, I didn't realize how much of a mess I was at the time. I thought I had it all together—a busy work schedule, daily writing sessions, weeknight plans with friends, and a seemingly contented demeanor.

I thought if I acted like everything was okay, I would believe that I was okay.

You came along at precisely the best and worst times. I needed a distraction, a reason to regularly check my phone and indulge in endless conversation—anything to escape the clamor of my mind.

I liked the attention. The random *thinking of you* morning texts and the late hours into the afternoon where you'd indulge me with the indelicate details of your mind. I played into it well, and you enjoyed playing the game.

Our moments together were brief enough for no one to be curious about where you'd been. I remember you'd pick me up, and I'd be anxious on our drive, my fingernails digging into the worn-out leather of your passenger seat. I'd smile at your tacky jokes and stare out the window, calculating how many years your personality added to your age.

I'm sure you thought you were slick, a man fifteen years my

senior flirting with the bartender he never thought he'd be sitting parallel to in his car. You feigned spontaneity when you'd come up with random weekday plans, but after a few weeks, I caught on to your estimations and manipulations. Nothing was ever impromptu and on a whim. You were too mundane for that.

Before you'd drop me off, you'd take one final glance in the rearview mirror, verifying that everything looked the way it did before leaving. No red remnants on the borders of your lips. I'd get out of the car, a stale aftertaste lingering in the air.

The last time I saw you, I wondered if you knew it too. The impression you left. The lies I unraveled.

The sour remnants of a man consumed in his own web, unable to think of anyone other than the person staring back at him in the rearview mirror.

Love,
DANIELLE

A LASTING FIRST IMPRESSION

Dear Aaron,

I saw you from across the bar. Your long hair was tucked behind your ears with a few strands masking your eyes. You were playing pool with a girl you came out with, both of you focusing on the movement of the ball when it was your turn.

I was on vacation in Los Angeles, sitting with friends in the corner booth and watching. I pointed you out to them, noticing how the light above the pool table accentuated your cheekbones and how when you smiled, your eyes intensified.

I had a few drinks and felt bold, maybe a little cocky, too. I turned to my friends and told them that I knew I was going to kiss you that night.

We both got up to order drinks at the same time and landed side by side, our elbows on the cold marble bar. You told me you liked the song on the jukebox and then asked if I was from LA, saying I didn't look like a California girl. I told you I was from New York and was in town for the next week visiting family. You said that this was your favorite bar to go to with friends.

Our small talk turned into meaningful conversation before we returned to our opposite corners. Every couple of minutes, I would glance over and catch your eyes on mine. You'd grin, and I'd smile back. As the end of the night grew closer, I watched you leave with the girl you were with.

My friends and I ordered another round of drinks and continued our conversation, but I still thought of you and our small yet substantial interaction.

A few moments later, you walked back into the bar alone, searching for me. Our eyes met and you walked over to our table, introducing yourself to everyone and asking if you could take a seat.

There were people all around us, the music was roaring, and the lights were bright, but our eyes never drifted. No matter how much noise there was, I still only heard your voice. No matter how many others were around me, it felt like you still only saw me.

That's how I like to remember you, Aaron.

As the guy who came back to the bar to kiss the girl from New York, to leave a lasting first impression of a night out with a stranger.

Love,
DANIELLE

A DIFFERENT TYPE OF ACHE

Dear Carter,

Out of all the men who said they didn't want to end up in my writing, I never thought you would be one of them. If our thirteen-year-old selves peered into the future, they wouldn't believe that we don't speak anymore. I'm still finding it hard to believe. Sometimes this silence feels like one big joke, and I'm just waiting for you to call me and tell me you're kidding. That you miss me too. That you've been dying to talk again.

I have to correct myself when I mention us in the present tense. I don't think I'll ever get used to it, but the more time passes that we don't speak, I realize I'll have to learn to live with it.

There's not a day that goes by when I don't think about you. My memory is spiteful that way. Some days I remember us in the tenth grade; how we'd pretend Tuesdays were Fridays and drink Bud Lights in my room while filming pseudo-Nickelback music videos with my camcorder. Other days I see us as twenty-year old's walking hand in hand in Belfast, drunk or hungover, simulating our best versions of an Irish brogue. Then, as the projector of my mind switches slides, we're lying in bed in our underwear on Sunday morning, laughing with tears in our eyes as we recount everything that transpired the night before.

How could our relationship be so rare yet so easily fade

away? I catch myself wondering if our connection was real. My mind acts like a detective, retracing our every step to spot holes in our narrative, to catch us in our lie. Maybe if I could pinpoint the falsities earlier in our history, it wouldn't sting so bad not to have you in my life anymore.

Last summer was the hardest season of my life, and I often wonder if it was painful for you too. I wrote you a letter to tell you how abandoned I felt; how missing you caused physical aches. I spent so much time trying to compose the perfect words to explain how much I needed you again. I remember waiting for your response all day, and when I finally heard your voicemail, it was the first time I recognized that it wasn't you who was speaking. The person I had known for most of my life was absent. Your voice was robotic and distant, and your response read like an emotionless script.

I stayed in bed the entire night after listening to your message, trying to ignore what my instincts were telling me. *This is over. He's not the same. You'll never go back to the way things were before.* But I'm learning over and over in the most colorful of ways that my intuition is never wrong. Still, I like to live on the outskirts of my senses and pretend this is just a hiatus in our seventeen-year-long friendship.

The other night, for the first time in a long time, I allowed myself to scroll back through our texts from the last two years. I was hoping to create a villain out of you, the way you did to me, so I could put this to bed and not think about you anymore. What I uncovered made me feel worse, though, because hidden within your texts was the message I never allowed myself to read.

It's not that you're an awful person. You just didn't value our friendship as much as I did. It's not that you changed for the worse; it's that you'd rather let silence rip us apart than confront conflict head-on. And it's not that you're a bad friend; it's that you'd rather surround yourself with people who think like you, so it's easier to be a good friend to them.

What does that make you to me, though?

Do you know what keeps me up at night? The memory of the person I always knew and the fear that I'll never see him again. If ten years down the road we bumped into each other and took our chance at closure, would I ever see the friend who was once my home again?

I thought I was good at forgiving people, but I'm having a hard time making amends with you. Broken hearts heal easier when you're angry, and lately, I breach the border of indifference. I think you live here, too, because if you felt a fraction of how I feel, you'd be standing at my door trying to fight for what we had.

But stay where you are; it's safe there with no one to question your mindset, why you do the things you do, or believe what you believe. Shallow waters surround you when there's nothing holding a mirror to your face.

One text that stood out among the others, just before things changed, was after you listed fifteen of our friendship's funniest moments. You said, *Thanks for having the best memories stored in this brain.*

Was it just our humor that was real and nothing deeper?

I wonder how you remember me now. Did you delete all the voicemails I left you at 4 a.m. when I lived in Las Vegas? Am I still the only person to take up space in your inbox? Or have you erased those memories to avoid looking back, admitting you're wrong, so you can continue your new life without me?

Heartbreak isn't new territory, but this is a different type of ache. Out of everyone who's hurt me, I never thought you were capable of deserting me too. It's the loneliest type of rejection and the sharpest isolation I've ever felt.

So, sometimes I let my heart take a backseat, and I allow my mind to play our friendship's montage on the big screen, tracing back to the day we met in the seventh grade, up to the last genuine text you sent me. And I drift there for a while, hoping that maybe I'll wake up and this was all just a dream.

But my phone still isn't ringing, and my door has no one knocking on it. It's only me here, waiting for a reunion I'm realizing will never come to be.

Love,
DANIELLE

IT'S YOUR TURN

Have you ever written a letter to an ex-boyfriend, girl-friend or friend? Have you ever written a letter with no intention of sending it? When I wrote these letters, I knew I was writing them for myself and no one else. It was a therapeutic outlet and creative prompt, although I have used this practice in the past with the intention of eventually sending the letters.

Alanis Morrisette released a song, "Unsent," in 1998 that I listened to a lot as a teenager. I remember sitting around the bulky Dell computer that my family shared and watching the music video for it with Carter. We thought it was such a great representation of the song lyrics and would say to each other, "This is the best song ever created!"

I laugh now thinking of those Friday nights, but that song is what originally prompted me to write letters to my exes. Often there are many things left unsaid at the end of a relationship. There's so much that we hold inside that feels lighter once we release it—whether someone else is receptive to it or not.

Grab your journal and choose someone from your past to write a letter to. This can be a former romantic partner, friend, family member, or someone deceased. Say every-thing that you never said to this person. Be detail-oriented and specific about your history and the emotions you felt then and now. Don't be afraid to tap into the depth of your truth.

The deeper you go, the more powerful this practice is, and the more you'll release.

Our pain is the greatest portal to our healing.

SEPTEMBER

I think of you in September when the wind carries its first chill and summer's far behind me. Something about the leaves turning marigold and the days getting shorter brings me back to you.

I write in bed most nights with candles lit and windows open as I gaze out to the sky. Fall lifts itself through the screen, brushing goosebumps on my skin, and I remember the night we stayed up until 5 a.m. on the beach, chilly and damp with a single blanket around us. You said you loved how I laugh at my own jokes, and I told you I was both nervous and desirous of something eternal.

You didn't know how to say you were looking for that too. You couldn't find the words to express that you've been searching for years and hoped this was it.

September's here again, and I remember you, that night on the beach, and all the words left unsaid. I wonder where you are and how you're doing—if you've discovered what your heart was hungry for.

I can tell you this: I'm still somewhere in between, sitting in the corner chair of a waiting room, not yet recognized.

Can you be found when you're not entirely lost?

Can you fall in love when your heart no longer seeks affection?

I think of you in September, and I remember your eyes, cerulean, peering into mine. I hope you're somewhere warm and dry on a beach with a woman looking back at you, knowing that you're where you're meant to be.

Sitting next to the one you've been waiting for.

THE SIGNIFICANCE OF TIME

Is there a month that holds significance in your life? Who or what does it remind you of? What memories rise to the forefront when you think of that month and why?

Get your journal and start writing about the first month that pops into your mind and the significance it holds for you. What happened during this month? Did you fall in love? Did your heart get broken? Did you battle the largest challenge of your life? Did you unleash your inner strength?

Whatever it is that happened, write about the imagery, experiences, people, and emotions of that month. Let your feelings guide the pen. Allow your memories to lead the way.

WHERE DID YOU GO?

Where did you go when I left?

An apartment that was once a home became vacant, dim, and stripped of my memory.

Where did you go when you saw the void?

Sleepless nights waiting for a light to radiate on the nightstand next to my bed, to see your name on a screen with a message for me.

Another restless night, another wet pillow, another morning met with swollen eyelids. Can you measure how much you mean to a person by their response to you leaving?

I was overwhelmed with underwhelm. Like a tide that comes in high just to level out before it nears you, I was left waiting for the storm to surge, the waves to rise, the current to take me out and away with it, but it was only me standing on the shore, smooth waters around me.

I thought I'd leave a trail of reckless abandonment. A fire blazing, burning, and smoldering behind me. What I imagined would be a wakeup call for you turned into a harsh awakening for me.

Tears streaming down flushed cheeks, breath short and stuttered, unable to speak. Wasn't that enough for you to see me? Wouldn't that have been a good time to recognize what had brought us to this place?

But you still got on the plane. You still chose to leave.

Maybe you thought I'd be waiting for you when you got home. Maybe you imagined our conversation being wiped clean. My words had never amounted to action before; why would it be different this time?

More than anything else, what haunts me now is how there was no fight to be won for you. No charge forward to change what broke us. No looking in the mirror and taking responsibility for the ending to our story.

You never thought this would be our collapse. You believed you would write the final chapters. Looking back now, I see our paths split long before I left.

I started walking in a different direction every time you chose yourself over me. I began running during the nights I woke up every hour to an empty space beside me. I was miles ahead of you on the morning I woke up to no one there.

How could you not see that I was already gone before I left? How couldn't you know that you were the one pushing me away?

My leaving wasn't abrupt. It was slow and steady, calm and collected, unshakeable and resolute.

You couldn't see me.

I don't think you ever did.

Tapping into Your Anger

Can you turn your anger with someone or something into a poem, journal entry, letter, or song lyrics? Is there anger that lingers within you from a long time ago that would feel better if released?

When we can transform our pain—especially anger—into art, it not only helps us relax in the present moment, but also offers us the space to heal. You don't have to consider yourself an artist to create art. You can express yourself through any artistic modality you feel called to. Write, draw, paint, sing, dance, act—practice whatever type of art you want. It's not about creating something perfect. It's the act of transmuting your anger into art that's beautiful.

GLASS HOUSE

I have this dream that visits me some nights.
  I'm standing in a glass house looking out to the sea.
  Clouds like oyster shells hover overhead, and waves the size of skyscrapers begin to rise.

I look around, and as everyone scatters to escape, I'm stuck standing, facing the flood coming for me.

Waters once bruised blue are washed white, swelling higher to reach the sky.

As glass shatters and the ocean roars over me, I become one with the storm and float driftless, breathless, lifeless, under water.

I wonder if this is a metaphor for how I felt with you, my love.

When I couldn't remove my eyes from the impending danger.

When I wouldn't move until I was forced by a power greater than me.

When I waited until the very last moment for my heart to be as fragile as glass.

When I allowed you to break me.

HE VISITS ME WHEN
I SLEEP

He visits me when I sleep,
in the sacred slumber
where worlds collide.

I wonder if our spirits
long for connection
in the ethereal
when our bodies
are separated
in human time.

Maybe our souls
desire intimacy
even in their
ripe perfection.

Maybe
our highest selves,
the awakened,
still crave warmth.

When I close my eyes
each night,
my heart swells
with yearning,
like a captain
anxiously seeking

refuge in violent,
turbulent storms.
I call for him
across vast
and desolate seas.

I reach for him
until I feel his hands
on mine.
When his fingers
trace the lineage
of my palms,
and his eyes
rest their gaze
on my emerald
greens,
I'm safe.

What do I do
with my waking hours
when I can't see
or touch him?
How do I continue forward
knowing that we'll never
again be?

I live for my dreams.

The seconds,
the passing blip,
the echoes,
the reflection
of a life
that only exists
in my memories.

If memories transform
into dreams
then keep me here

where sleeping is eternal
and waking is the dream.
I'll rest in my hibernation.

Does he too
see our nightly encounters,
the escape from daylight
and normal, daily doings,
our flight
into everlasting union,
a paradise
we couldn't recognize
here?

Does he too
wish he could go back
and change
what broke us —
what turned us
into two lost lovers,
sleeping and waking,
remembering and dreaming,
destined to always
be alone?

TO LOVE YOURSELF

S ometimes I wish I knew what you were doing. My mind traces back to us and I imagine you sitting in your apartment and looking around the freshly painted walls, realizing one of your dreams has come true. You're happy, you have most of what other men desire, yet there's a desertedness inside you that you don't know how to fill.

I always tried to pour myself into you to fill any gaps or holes. I wanted to meet you there, where all your hunger and thirst for what you didn't understand was quenched. I always hoped you would rise to the person I know you wanted to be. I waited for that man to greet me with eyes open and aware, to feel his arms wrapped like a blanket around me.

I caught glimpses of this version of us. The Sunday afternoons we spent on the couch, our bodies entwined, hands united, laughter ascending from our bellies, eyes meeting each other's just long enough to express sincere gratitude for the life we shared. Mornings where we held each other a little longer than normal. Nights where your chest was my pillow and your voice a lighthouse, directing me home.

Maybe one day I will meet the man who can always be this way. Maybe at some point, we'll discover in each other what once kept us close.

But you're in a city with new people. You'll be catching the eyes of women all around you, and you'll let one of them inside. She won't be meeting the man I knew, though. She may never meet that man, for he's been out-grown, torn down, and replaced.

The man she'll be meeting, the person she'll fall in love with, is the man you couldn't be for me. He's the man you'll become because of me.

I can't picture it. I don't want to. But I hope when that day comes, you're happy, and she makes you happy.

I needed you to be someone you weren't willing to be, and I wonder if my leaving is what you needed.

To find yourself.

To become yourself.

To love yourself.

YOU ARE A TEACHER

Whether you're aware of this or not, you are a teacher. You have taught friends, family, coworkers, classmates, and romantic partners lessons that have helped them along their paths. These lessons are not always taught intentionally but are learned from living alongside one another.

When I find it difficult to move through a breakup or reflect on my experiences with a loving perspective, I try to remember everything I learned from my past relationships and everything I taught someone else. By looking at your past through the lens of what you gained and shared, rather than what you lost, you tap into the essence of human existence.

We are here to learn and grow from each other. When we can reflect on our romantic relationships in this way, we recognize that every person serves a purpose in our lives, just as we serve a purpose in other people's lives. Doesn't this perspective feel better than reflecting on our pasts with bitterness or regret?

What lessons have you taught others?

What would an ex-boyfriend or girlfriend say they learned from you?

What characteristics of your personality teach others the most?

What is the greatest lesson you unintentionally taught someone else?

What impact do you want to make on others?

A LIFE BEYOND DOUBT

He wasn't aware of how he affected me.
I don't think he knew how that single
flick of his eyelids,
his fingers running through my hair,
his knee gently grazing mine,
surged a current in my veins.

He has an intense delicacy to him,
a mysterious yet inviting demeanor
where I want to be led into his world
but also kept on the outskirts,
to maintain this distance that feeds us;
the space that nurtures the connection
we share; where nothing is permanent—
the present is all there is.

There's something to be said
about the ephemeral.

I live in evanescence.
It's safe here.
I like the familiar.
With no attachments
comes more security
and I am secure
in myself.

But I catch myself daydreaming lately
and he's always there.

My feet want to tread the winding trail
that leads to his doorstep.
My hands want to knock
and be welcomed inside.
My lips want to ladle the curve of his neck
and taste his sweetness.
My waist wants to be grasped by
covetous fingers and be firmly held.
My eyes want to be seen in darkness
and understood in the light.
My heart wants to be loved rarely,
tenderly, and with care.

I want this
in moments
of blossomed arousal and heat.
But I know these temptations
are only born
from what can never fully be,
and I'm beginning to wonder
if these momentary appetites
serve their own kind of feast,
and if they're the only type
I'll ever get to eat.

He lives in similar ways
and realizes the beauty
in the temporary,
which is why we recognize
ourselves in each other.

But can there be more,
even in the fleeting?
Is there a chance
of stability
even among the fear

of permanence?

The transitory nature of my life
and my clinging to the short term
are momentary
and fading.

Maybe I want more.
Maybe there's a life
beyond my doubt
waiting for me.

How will I ever know
if I don't tell him?

How will I find love
if I don't try?

YOUR LOVE IS WITHIN MEDITATION

Listen to this poem on **Struck Inside Out's** *website. See "Additional Resources" at the end of the book for the link to access it.*

Here we are again,
another ending.
A sweet beginning too.

You didn't lose
yourself in love.
The time you shared
wasn't wasted.

Yes, your expectations
weren't met.
Yes, you thought
it was the "real thing."

But is it okay to return
to yourself?
Maybe *you*
are what you need?

I know your heart
is hurting.

I know you don't want
to be here again.

But you've already
explored these caverns.
You understand
what it's like to bleed.

Your grief
softens you.
Your wounds
become your wisdom.

What you see now
is because of your past.
Heartache offers
insight into clearer decisions.

Feel what you need to.
Process what you must.

Remember,
endings aren't failures.
The act of trying
is what counts.

You're now stronger
and wiser.
You know more about
what you want.

How does that happen
without taking chances?
How do you learn
without losing?

Old doorways
are shut,
and that's okay.

You'll open the right ones.

Trust your timing.
Honor your path.
The love that's meant for you
can never miss you.

Your heartbreak
is the portal for you
to discover more.
Love yourself more.

Isn't that the point?
We always return
home to ourselves
at the end of the day.

Take a deep breath.
Love who you are,
where you are,
and *why* you are here.

When you love yourself
for yourself and nothing else,
the love you are seeking
finds you.

For it already was,
and always will be,
within.

NURTURING YOUR
HOME BASE

S elf-love is a journey that never ends. Like everything else in life, just when we think we've learned all that we can absorb, a new lesson languidly unravels like the silky petals of a peony. Isn't that beautiful? We are *always* learning.

Love teaches us the most because it hurts us the most. To fall in love and hand your trust over to someone is like pulling your heart from your chest and placing it directly in their hands. Your heart is no longer yours. The thrill of that can feel exhilarating. The aftermath of it can be arduous.

Yet, we give love another chance because the rush and pleasure of letting someone into our worlds always outweigh the agony of losing them. The lessons always eclipse any regret.

Whether you were with your partner for three weeks or three years, time is never wasted. Whether you knew that person wasn't right for you from the beginning, or you only realized they weren't a good fit until the very end, you still grew as a result of being with them. Whether your relationship ended in marriage, divorce, or having children, the end result is not always what counts. A relationship's success doesn't equate to long-term plans. Relationships are worth investing in because whatever the final result is, you walk away stronger, smarter, and brighter for having been in it.

If you can learn to return home to yourself with a compassionate heart regardless of what your past relationship's outcome is, then you'll know that you're always deserving of love—even if that's your own love. The periods of solitude between relationships are a sacred space that should be valued and not ignored. Your solitude is where your most important relationship is nurtured. Embrace alone time rather than dread it. If you have a stable relationship with yourself, then no matter where you are, who you're with or not with, you'll always have a loving home base to return to.

PLANNING A DAY FOR YOURSELF

Have you ever taken yourself on a date? Do you go to restaurants, movies, or parks alone? Do you feel comfortable sitting at your favorite restaurant and eating dinner by yourself? Would you go to a movie you've been wanting to see in your own company? Would you plan a solo beach day to start the book you've been meaning to read?

I personally love doing things alone. I never used to be like this, but over time I've become someone who doesn't need the company of others to be fulfilled. Of course, I love spending time with family, friends, and partners, but I don't need to squeeze noise into every moment of silence. And I like that when I spend time alone, I get to do things that I love without having to address anyone else. It's the most freeing feeling!

The time that I spend by myself is valuable and something I treasure. Each week I carve out time for solitude because those moments refuel me to be social. My solitude feeds my social life and vice versa.

Grab your journal and map out a day for just yourself. If you don't want to spend an entire day alone, plan a solo date for a few hours. What's something you've been wanting to do but haven't gotten around to? What is one place you've been meaning to visit that your friends or family aren't interested in going to? What is an activity that nurtures your soul? What is a skill you want to learn? How will coming home to yourself feel if you do it weekly, monthly, or yearly? And *why* are you choosing to create more space for solitude? What are you hoping to gain from it?

When you plan your alone time, only schedule things that you genuinely feel excited to do. Your alone time doesn't have to take you somewhere outside, either. Maybe you just want to meditate, watch a movie, or write in your journals at home. Whatever your desires are, listen to them and honor them. You can't go wrong with planning this. The more time you spend with yourself at home or on personal dates, the more you'll enjoy your own company.

So, make a list of all the activities you'd love to do with just yourself. Write down *why* you want to do them and how you want to feel *while* you're doing them. Create intentions for why you're choosing solitude. Jot down a few words that represent the emotions you'd like to embody when you're on your own.

Your alone time is some of the most valuable time you'll ever have. Learn to love it and watch as the rest of your relationships begin to flourish.

CHAPTER 8
POEMS ON LOVE AND LOSS

Dear Reader,

If you haven't noticed by now, I love to write about love.

Love is beautiful.
Love is messy.
Love is exciting.
Love is difficult.
Love is magic.
Love is solid.
Love is bliss.
Love is heartbreak.
Love is patience.
Love is obsession.
Love is listening.
Love is ignoring.
Love is passion.
Love is disastrous.
Love is understanding.
Love is mysterious.
Love is harmony.
Love is imbalance.
Love is compassion.
Love is war.
Love is wanderlust.

Love is home.

Love is our greatest teacher.

Sending love always,
DANIELLE

ALL I'VE EVER KNOWN

What if I told you that I've never found home?

What if I said that I've always felt alone?

Even when held in warm hands
and looked at like gold.

Is it possible to be loved
and still unknown?

Will you ever see me
without being shown?

Can you love me
like it's all you've ever known?

I Hope to Live by the Sea

I hope one day
to live by the sea.
If not the sea,
then a garden.
If not a garden,
then nestled in the woods.

Trees as my protectors.
Cardinals, robins, and the white-tailed deer,
my neighbors.

A reticent stillness to welcome me
every day
into the beauty
of my life.

I would be content with this —
a cottage camouflaged in vines,
furtive pathways toward the silky pond,
a night sky drenched in starlight.

I wouldn't need to return
to the world of
doing and producing.

All I need is this:

fertile soil
cold rain
fiery sunlight
petite seedlings
virginal sprouting
newborn greenery
fecund pastures
deep inhales
longer exhales
twilight's alchemy
earth's infinite ceiling
this world in all its wonder.

Yes, a return to the sacred.

WHAT ARE YOUR HOPES?

We all have dreams for the type of love we want to experience. We may envision an ideal partner or the qualities of a relationship we want to have. Outside of those aspirations, what does the natural world offer you that fills your world with beauty and romance? How does nature reflect your desires? Is it the way nature takes her time yet still gets everything done? Is it the transformation from seedling to dahlia? What does nature teach you about your dreams and desires?

I Want a Lover

I want a lover.

A lover who not only sees me
but knows me.

The way that flower
knows its root.

The way the moon
knows its luminescence.

The way those birds
know the current of the wind.

I want someone to peel me open
like the skin of an orange,
the flesh of its shell

and drink me whole.

I want a lover
who digs into me

with hands scouring hills,
fingernails laden in lust,
lips wet with hunger,
eyes wide open.

I want this

the way you want me.
I see this
from the longing in your eyes.

The way your tongue
licks your lips.

How you harbor
a sadness inside.

I'm still waiting for you
to show me
what it's like to be known.
How it feels to be seen.

And I want you,
and only you,
to show me.

MEET ME THERE

I asked you
to touch me.

Not just with your hands.

Your fingers
grazing up and down
the crest of my navel.

Linger there.

Arousing goosebumps.

Spreading like wildfire.

Surging flushed skin.

Your breath is
morning dew
as your lips
circuit my ear.

Breathing is
deepening.

Heart is
galloping.

Mouth is

on mine.

I want you
to look at me.
Don't close
your eyes.

Ascending higher,
together we come
crashing down.

Stay with me.
Steady your gaze.

Don't sink
lower now.

Keep searching.

Continue looking.

Forever unraveling.

There
you'll find me.

Between the clamor,
underneath the rough,
just over the peak,
beyond the surface.

Meet me there.

WHEN I SAW YOU THE OTHER DAY

When I saw you the other day,
I didn't know what to say,
except I hope you're happy.

It's funny, isn't it?
How you can know a person
inside and out.

The inner stirrings of their heart,
the way their chest rises and falls
while they're sleeping,
the noises they make
when in a deep rest,
how their face bends
when angry,
and softens with laughter,
yet when your time
together is over,
you resort back
to being strangers
in front of each other.

As though the story
you had written together
never happened.

As though the love you shared

never existed.

It makes me sad to think of us
in this way.

To be seeing but not acknowledging.
To be present but not awake.
To be feeling but not expressing.

I wondered what you were thinking,
if you wanted to look my way,
but were afraid our eyes would meet
and the deep dive of your heart
plummeting straight into your stomach,
a kind of ache you weren't willing to brace.

I think of you sometimes,
and wonder how you are,
if your life is moving along
as you always hoped it would.

Sometimes it still feels strange
not being part of your world,
the moments that lift you up,
excite you,
amaze you,
and the ones that pull you
deeper,
down,
darker,
into the heaviness of it all.

I saw you the other day
and didn't know what to say,
my heart was beating faster than normal.
But I wanted you to know
that I hope you're in a good place,
and I hope life is treating you well.

I hope you're happy.

WISH SOMEONE WELL

When we run into an ex-boyfriend or girlfriend that we haven't seen in a while, our hearts can feel as though they have stopped beating for a moment. Then, in a sudden surge, our hearts race against our chests. Emotions get dusted from their creaky shelves, and what we thought we didn't feel anymore is alive and breathing within us.

Write a poem about this sensation. Write about the rush you experience when seeing someone from your past. Write about the dormant emotions that awaken just by locking eyes with this person.

Are you able to wish this person well?

Can you send love their way?

Can you be at peace with your ending?

EPHEMERAL LOVE

Why can't I love you now
in this way
even if we both know
we're not the other's
person?

Why do we always
have to have
an always?

What about now?
What about here?
What about the temporary?

A fleeting love.

A love that doesn't rise above.
Fall
below.
Make your heart shatter
or earth shake.

No expectations.
No foreseeable future.

Just here.
Just now.
Just this.

Can we
just have
this?

THE BEAUTY IN THE TEMPORARY

What is something in your life that's valuable because of its temporality? How is this person, experience, or thing beautiful because of its transient nature? Can you love its impermanence and see the significance in what's short-lived?

WILDFIRE

I've been pushing and pulling
against myself again.

I've become both
the raft and the tsunami.
A torrent of waves
crushing me
underneath
the surface.

Yet,
I always become
the life vest.

Eventually I rise
anew,
refreshed,
awakened.

It's not you
who does this
to me.
It's my own doing
or undoing.

You lit the match
and now I'm on fire.
Burning,
blazing,

aflame.

And you can never
dim my light
again
because those who only
fuel their own spark
can never fully blaze.

You taught me how to burn
on my own.

What was once a flicker
in your eyes
is now a wildfire.

Ebullient and unrestrained.

BIRD WITHOUT WINGS

What is it like?
She said,
to fly above,
among,
and below
the clouds?

How does it feel
when the wind
nudges your back
and the sun
spills over
your hair?

What do you think
when you peer
underneath
and see that
you're merely
a tiny echo
chanting across skies?

Tell me what I must become
to pivot in flight
the way you do.

How can I be
like you,
sweet bird?

How do I
teach myself
to soar
even when
I have forgotten
that I too
was born
with wings?

THE GHOST OF ME

I've thought of it before.

How she'd look beside you.
What color her eyes would be.
If her hair would be as long as mine.
If she could make you laugh like me.

Would you love her the same?
Would you love her more?
Would you remember me?

One day,
when you're in a new country,
watching royal ocean waves,
setting sights on bluer skies,
trying foreign foods,
and she is next to you,
you'll get a glimpse
into our history
and wonder what this landscape
would be like if you were with me.

You'll remember how my eyes
on yours made your heart broaden.
How my hands around your pelvis
and my lips on your shoulders
once felt like home.

How when I woke up beside you,

eyelids still dozy,
arms and legs not quite awake,
I'd reach for you.

How when lying in bed
in the black of night
my mouth would trace
the center of your throat,
down the crest of your chest,
toward the smooth skin
beneath,
and pleasure
would awaken.

And you'll think to yourself,
Will it always be this way?

Will I always be in the background
of your new world
with your new women
in far and distant places
to chase away
the ghost of me?

Will I ever be free
of her memory?

That's the thing about our pasts;
we can travel to opposite
corners of the globe
to meet as many strangers
as we desire,
to saturate our hearts
for a single night,
all to forget our history.

But what was real,
and never let you down —
what made you feel the most alive

can never be erased.

In your pursuit
to wipe out my memory,
you're throwing wood to the fire.
Adding embers to the flames.

You're remembering me now
but with a vision
only hindsight delivers.
You can't understand
how you didn't love me
more before.

But now is not before,
and it's too late.

You Are the Moth, I Am the Flame

I've met your kind before.
Dark and hollow.
Predictable yet intriguing.

It always seems authentic
when it begins.

The right words,
gestures,
movements,
and glares
roll off
you
as though
we were meant to be.

But there's always that moment
when you shift gears
and the light
hits your face
in just the right way
where I can see
that you're not good
for me.

Even when truth is born
I still find ways

to make myself stay.

To believe the lie
and think that I
can change you.

Why do I always
want to change you?
How is it your kind
that finds me?
What is it about me
that wishes
to fix
the broken?

Maybe I'm broken too.

Maybe you see your other half
in me.

But I'm no half.
No smaller part
of a whole.

I am
the whole
thing.

You're the moth.
I'm the flame.
And I'm learning
to burn everything
that no longer
serves me.

BURN AND RELEASE

Get a piece of paper and write about someone or something that you want to release. This can be something tangible in your life or emotions, patterns, attachments, and addictions that you want to let go of. Write in detail about what you want to release and be free from. Wish this person, thing, or emotion well, and thank it for what it's taught you. Write: "I release myself from _____. Thank you for teaching me _____. I will carry these new lessons with me. I no longer need _____. I set myself free."

You can keep a copy of this in your journal or take the piece of paper outside and light a match to it. As the paper burns, imagine the energy of what you want to release drifting up and away. Imagine yourself free. Envision yourself walking down a new path. Smile, place both hands on your heart, and set a new intention for yourself.

Declare: "I am _____."

Thank yourself for releasing what no longer serves you. Honor yourself for creating space to bring in the new.

WITH THE SNOWFALL

I thought of you this morning
with the snow falling
softly, tranquilly, quietly.
My blanket
wrapped around me
as the glacial air
filtered the room.

If I was still with you,
you'd be on the couch
in the living room
on the phone
talking about business.
Your pen in hand,
laptop open,
serious and focused.

Our bedroom, my solitude,
not just separated from you,
but a loneliness,
a steady desertion from
the unified existence,
the connecting thread
that weaves everything together.
A kind of love I always craved.

Why when I left bed
to come out and see you
with a smile on my face,

arms yearning for your warmth,
would you turn the other way?
Why when I wanted simple affection
would you retreat to work,
instead of the woman in front of you
who gave you the love
you never had
yet always wanted?

Snow fallen days were icy outside
but our apartment was colder.
I can still feel the frost of disconnect
while sitting on opposite ends
of the couch.

Looking over at you,
your eyes on the TV
or the screen in your hand,
and my mind would wander
outside to the sparrows
sitting on the large oak tree,
imagining what life would be like
if I listened to myself,
the stirrings of my instincts,
the guiding light that's ceaselessly
leading me
to where I must go,
to whom I'm destined to be.

I look out
toward snowy landscapes
and the choir of birds,
a family together
among branches
in the old pine tree,
and even though
I'm now alone,
I've never felt
in better company.

A COLD NIGHT FOR NOVEMBER

You asked me to drive you home
after having too much to drink.
Your eyes held mine
both playful and mournful,
like a little boy
who dirtied himself
and got in trouble.

It was a cold night for November.
Our mouths blew out
milky clouds
as we listened to
The Black Keys
on the five-minute ride
to your house.

We spoke of menial things;
our plans for the week,
and how we already
couldn't wait for summer.
I'd be on the beach
down south
with family
the following day,
and wouldn't want to
return to New York.

I wish I could escape
sometimes too,
you said.

Bulky oak trees
whose barren arms
stretched toward
a black sky
bordered our drive.
Tiny boxes
like dominoes
lined the street,
housing clandestine stories,
fragmented dreams,
unspoken longings –
parallel lives.

How easy it could be
for one to fall
over
and topple
the other,
until nothing remained
but the broken
bones of a home.

As we neared your house,
you told me to pull over.

Just for a minute.

You stared at me
seriously, somberly –
a fertile intensity.

Leaning over,
you wove your hands
through my hair,
tugging at its dusky roots,

pulling me closer.

Your tongue grazed
my lips
then
tasted my ear,
down my neck,
until your mouth
feasted on the valleys
beneath.

We shouldn't be doing this.
Please stop.

I've wanted this.
Keep going.

I drove away
knowing we could never
go back.
We would never
be the same.

But your memory
is like a flickering
light in my mind.

As soon as I
turn off the switch,
one beams,
your amber eyes,
then another,
your pliant mouth,
then a third,
how you said,
I need you.

I don't know why
you still drift

like a balmy breeze
steadily hitting
the doorway
of my heart
when I'm trying
to keep this door
permanently shut.

Is it wrong
to say that I hope
thoughts of me
keep you up
at night, too?

Is it sad to admit
that I wonder
what could have been
if we met
at a different time?

If our lives
crossed paths
just seconds before
someone else
called you *mine*?

Do you ever
think about it too?

Or is it only me
living in this dream?

RETURN TO THE SACRED

I woke up today and felt the same
as I did yesterday,
and the day before that, too.

For a sliver of a moment,
a fraction of a second,
like the sun flashing brightly
blinding me of any view,
I forgot everything.

I didn't think of the panic.
I wasn't focused on the uncertainty —
all the unpleasant images
our minds conceive
when faced with the unknown.

I didn't look for reasons to worry.
I wasn't trying to remember the last
piece of news I read.

I didn't think of the wrinkles on
my grandmother's forehead,
deepening,
weakening,
as the chaos grows louder.

I wasn't setting my eyes

on the possibility of infection
going viral
among myself,
my family,
or friends.

Instead,
in that brief space
between sleeping
and waking,
I opened my eyes
and saw beauty.

I saw love.

The sun's rays,
trickling in.
My plants sitting,
basking
in the light.

Birds outside
awakening,
nestling,
singing.
All because
they can.
All because
they want to.

The silence,
the breeze,
the delicate sensation
of spring dawning.

I remember now
what it was like
being a kid,
not yet having ears

attuned to the
loudness.
Not yet having eyes
seeking the negative.
Not yet having a heart
waiting for its next suffering.

I sat up in bed,
and with the steady
tiptoe of the world's reminders
settling in,
I remembered
the girl
from many years ago
who when blinded
from all crises
still chose to see the good,
the enchantment,
the possibility of magic,
as though
that's the only way
she knows how to be.
As though that's the only way
she should live.

We are being reminded
of our youth.
We are being transported
back to serenity.
We, our beings,
are being asked
to be.

Nothing more.
Simply the return
to our former ways of being.
When the world
wasn't about
the destination

and perpetual force forward,
but the unimaginable,
indescribable
beauty
that's ever-present,
when we allow ourselves
to sit
in the present.

Sit
in
the
present.

Allow yourself to be.

When all of this has passed,
and the wave of normalcy
returns,
you may find yourself
wishing for this
reprieve,
of a world not spinning
on its axis
for work, movement, travel,
constant motion,
eternal doing.

For once
in your life,
you're being
encouraged
to simply be.

That is all.

Simply be.

WHAT DID YOU LEARN?

What did the pandemic and quarantine teach you?

Were there positive experiences and revelations that took place during quarantine?

What are some things you would have never learned if it weren't for the pandemic?

What was the best thing that happened to you during 2020 and 2021?

How can you transform your pain and fear into strength and hope?

I know the pandemic took its toll on the world and left many with grief, loss, and sadness. Our world changed drastically within days and the fear that settled as a result left people feeling paralyzed.

Outside of the pain we collectively experienced, was there anything positive that came out of the pandemic? Is there insight you gained that you wouldn't have learned if it weren't for quarantine?

Write a list of everything positive that happened during this challenging time. List everything you learned *because* of the pandemic. Keep this list in your journal, or rip it out and put it on your nightstand to remind yourself of your strength in the darkest of times.

I REMEMBER

I saw a photo of you together
and was surprised
at how unsettled I felt.
Like the sharp edge of a knife
dragging itself through my ribs,
my heart bled for what was,
and all that's currently void.

Until now,
I didn't think I missed you.
Until a few moments ago,
I was satisfied on my own.
How could seeing your face
with someone new
erase all the growth
I've weathered?

You held her hand
with adoration.
Your smile was boyish
and honest.
Did you look
that elated with me?
Did you hold my hand
with such reverence and pride?
Do you love her more
than you loved me
in such a short span of time?

I'm the one who left.
You tried to fight for us again.
I told you it was too late.
I closed the door one last time.

It doesn't make my exit
any easier.
It doesn't make my decision
any less questionable.

The hardest part
wasn't the act of leaving.
It was after,
when the dust settled,
and my choices sunk in.
The silence
between what was
and what will be.
The late evening hours
when loneliness lurked
through my being.
When I stared restlessly
at the ceiling,
waiting for sleep
to consume me.

I remember the harsh pang
of learning to close my eyes
alone again,
of retraining my arms to embrace
the emptiness beside me
instead of your chest.
I remember telling myself
that everything would be okay
when my world
was falling apart.

I remember leaving you.
Waiting for you.

Marching forward.
Falling backward.
Uneasiness.
Regret.
Self-love.
Revival.

I will remember
my resilience
and inner guidance.
My descent into twilight
before burgeoning into blooms.

I will remember this,
when my mind only recalls
the romanticized story of us.
Not the underlying truth.

And when I remember,
I will wish you
and your new love well.

I'll remember the seed
that planted this long ago —
my soul's yearning for more,
my heart's hunger for pure love —
and I'll remember that by leaving
by choosing solitude,

I'm now ready.

PLANTING FLOWERS AS BEAUTIFUL REMINDERS

You'll need three to five glass mason jars for this practice.
You'll also need planting soil, rocks or glass stones, small
glass cork bottles (two inches in length), and flower seeds
(your choice of flowers).

Grab a few small pieces of paper and on each separate sheet, write about an experience you overcame that you didn't think you'd get through. Write about the strength you exhibited by remaining true to yourself. Write down everything you learned and gained from making hard decisions for your highest good. You can write this as a letter to yourself, a list of lessons you learned and wisdom you attained, or any other format you feel called to. Just make sure that the piece of paper you're using can fit into the glass cork bottles when folded.

When you've written down a few or all the major changes you made in your life and the obstacles you overcame, fold each piece of paper and enclose it in the mini glass cork bottle. After you've enclosed and protected your love notes, take some of the rocks or glass stones and cover the bottom of the mason jar with them. Then pour soil onto the rocks or stones to create a second layer. Place your mini glass cork bottle on top of the soil, and then pour more soil to cover the bottle. Next, sprinkle your flower seeds, and then continue to fill the jar to the brim with soil. Pour half of a cup of water to top everything off and place your jars in a sunny spot in your home.

As you nurture and care for your plants, they'll serve as reminders of your ability to blossom. When you see the seeds growing roots and the soil sprouting buds, you'll remember how you are like the seeds, roots, and bud. You are grounded, you are growing, and you are blooming.

The more you love and care for your plants, the more you nurture yourself. Your words of encouragement, perseverance, and hope are in those jars. Every time you see them, you'll see a part of yourself. The parts of you as strong as roots, as magical as seeds, and as promising as newborn buds.

FOR ME

My solitude consumes me
and there's no escape.

No arms to run into.
No eyes beaming into mine.
No one to share my thoughts with.
No one to call mine.

I miss you,
and I'm beginning to think
that I'll never get past us.
I'm worrying that you're
always going to be standing
at a distance,
as I try to live without you.

Have you already moved on?
Do you think of me?

I wish I didn't think about you
the way that I do,
but I do.

No one tells you
how hard it is
to let go of someone
when you're the one
choosing to let go.
No one prepares you

for the sadness that follows
walking away.

I'm supposed to feel better
by now.
If I was the one who broke us,
shouldn't I be content alone?
Am I crazy to long
for a life that I left?

I felt you in bed last night,
when desolation snuck in
at its normal hour.
I gazed into the darkness
and saw an outline
of your face
inching toward mine.
I pretended you were real.

I tried to imagine
what it would feel like
if you were lying
next to me again.
What I would whisper to you
in the night.
How my fingers would brush
your cheeks.
How I'd inhale your eyes.

Both the absence of you
and presence of you
make me lonely.

I'm still trying to figure out
how to stand on my own.
How to be happy alone.
I thought that I'd discover
myself by now,
but as I continue

without you,
I'm learning that
self-love takes time.
The only way to attain it
is to take your time.

As the seconds
span into minutes,
the minutes stretch into hours,
the hours turn into months,
and the months spread into years,
I'll remember to sit with my loneliness.
I'll learn to observe my seclusion.
I'll choose to love myself.

If I was lonely with you,
and I'm lonely with me,
the only way
to set myself free
is to allow myself to be.

Not for you,

but for me.

MY GREATEST LOVE

I caught a vision of you
in a meditation once.

You were standing
in a garden
of carmine daylilies,
lavender hydrangeas,
and peonies tinted
as pale as moths' wings.

Humbly confident,
you irradiated
a glow I'd never seen.

Your wholesome smile —
the edges
of your lips
snugged the arcs
of your cheeks,
and the hazel
lapped around
your pupils,
perched
underneath
your outstretched
lashes —
an image of beauty
I couldn't believe.

Everything I never imagined
for myself
you effortlessly possessed.
How you stood
comfortably,
assuredly,
without the need
for approval
or to be seen
by others.

You're complete
in your company.
The way a rose
in efflorescence
requires nothing
but herself to grow.

Opening my eyes
after ascending into
your dream,
I wondered if we
would ever meet.

Who was this person
staring at me?
Were you glancing
backward as I
breached forward?

I didn't understand then
that what separated us
was the lie of time.

I was neither here
nor there,
but with you,
beside you,
inside you,

for all of eternity.

I know now
that you weren't a fantasy.
The shimmer
from your radiance
has lit candles
along opaque paths
while you've patiently waited
for me.

You are my life's greatest
love story.

My heart's companion
and guide.

How couldn't I see
you were within
me all along?

PROMPTS AND AFFIRMATIONS FOR TRANSMUTING PAIN INTO STRENGTH

- What lessons did your last heartbreak teach you?
- How did love and loss teach you more about yourself, your standards, and your dreams?
- Did the lessons you learned surprise you in any way? Why or why not?
- Think about a past love who hurt you. Think about everything they represent to you. Whether you can forgive your past love or not, what did they teach you from being in a relationship with them? How did your triggers with this person become your teachers?
- Write an affirmation about your ability to love someone. Loving someone requires bravery and vulnerability, qualities to be proud of. For example: "It is safe for me to love others because I am always learning from every relationship I have."
- Write an affirmation about your ability to endure heartbreak. Getting your heart broken requires courage and patience which is something to honor about yourself. For example: "I trust in my ability to experience love and loss; love opens my heart and loss expands it even further."

- Personalize the following mantras. Write the mantra on a piece of paper or post-it and place it somewhere you'll see it daily. "I am _____, _____, and _____." "I can handle _____, because I am _____."
- Fill in the blanks of the following statements. "Love has taught me _____, because it _____." "Loss has taught me _____, because it _____." "I am grateful to have experienced _____, because it has helped me become _____." "Thank you for _____."
- Record yourself saying the following statements to yourself and play the recording throughout the day to create a self-love practice. "It is safe for me to love and be loved. I love how I love myself and others. I love and approve of myself. My relationship to myself serves every other relationship. I honor every relationship in my life as I learn and grow from them." Feel free to adjust these statements depending on what you want to work on.
- What are your greatest strengths? Where did they come from?
- What is your favorite thing about your relationship with yourself right now? How did this type of relationship come about?
- How has your relationship to yourself changed over time?
- What are three traits that you love about yourself and why? When did you acquire these traits?
- What is one characteristic of your relationship to yourself that you can always rely on and how does that help you value it?
- What is one piece of advice, encouragement, or support that you can offer yourself right now? How does it feel to give yourself the love you seek outside of yourself? Can you practice this act of kindness more often?

Beauty Awaits You

Dear Reader,

I hope you enjoyed this collection of poetry and prose as much as I loved compiling it for you.

If my twenty-two-year-old self were to read this book, she would be nervous yet eager to step into the next decade of her life. She would see the pain that she was bound to experience but also the unrelenting beauty awaiting her. She would be scared but hungry to tread forward. She would understand that life's most exquisite moments are accented by heartache.

If you live your life on the edge of fear, never moving forward to jump, you'll always stay where you are. Change, heartbreak, and loss are essential parts of the human experience; they make our existence mysterious and remarkable.

I hope the stories, confessions, and lessons from this book act as a catalyst for you to live your life beyond the edge of fear. Take risks, embrace your darkness, and let your heart be your guide. You can never go wrong when you listen to yourself, so listen to yourself.

Honor how far you've come. Celebrate where you currently stand. Revel in all the destinations you'll go.

Every version of yourself deserves your love.

Sending love always,
DANIELLE

ADDITIONAL
RESOURCES

www.struckinsideout.com/meditations

Join the Struck Inside Out community by signing up for
my mailing list at www.struckinsideout.com/subscribe and
following me on Instagram at @struckinsideout.

ACKNOWLEDGMENTS

Mom and Dad, to whom this book is dedicated. You are my rock. My biggest fans. My home. Thank you for reading everything I've ever shared without skimming. Thank you for printing my weekly newsletters for my mailing list and writing notes on them when you could have just emailed me your thoughts. Thank you for always believing in me. It's because of you that I am the person I am today. You are my life's most treasured gift. I love you more than words can say.

Kelley, thank you for being a constant source of truth, support, and encouragement throughout my life. You've been there for me through everything and have always lifted my perception of myself and my work with your pep-talks, random complimentary texts, or just letting me know how proud you are of me. Your insight on this book helped elevate its quality. I can't thank you enough for always being the best big sister I could ever ask for.

Tina, thank you for being there for me when I didn't know how to be there for myself. Thank you for showing me a strong example of what a soulful woman looks like. Thank you for reading my work, in all its beautiful and not-so-beautiful stages, and for encouraging me to keep going. Your bravery and fortitude inspire me to follow the same example. I am honored to call you my sister and beyond grateful for your eternal support.

Katie, how many late-night or early-morning texts have I sent asking you to check your email and tell me your thoughts on my writing? You told me to follow my heart and go with my gut. Thank you for reminding me that my words have value, my story is worth sharing, and that I can help people by remaining true to myself. I look forward to scheduling future book tours together!

Owen, my cousin and podcast producer. Thank you for making the meditations in this book and my podcast sound exactly how I wanted them to. Thank you for not laughing at my disorganized notes in the meditation scripts I randomly send you at such short notice. You are so talented, and I'm lucky to have you as part of the *Struck Inside Out* team. "I'm so struck!"

David Leiter, my pro-bono lawyer and good friend who edited my book proposal before I decided to self-publish. You taught me how to be a better writer without realizing you were doing so. Thank you for offering comic relief during my weekly meltdowns in my office. I know your jokes were more for you to escape my office than for my own benefit, but I love you for them all the same.

Amanda Cavanna, your friendship has brought more joy, value, and meaning to my life. Thank you for being a great friend while I was writing this book — especially when I disappeared into solitude for many months. Your random texts telling me how much you love my writing mean so much to me. Let's keep laughing at everything together.

My family and friends, who have been reading my writing for years and sent random acts of kindness while I was writing this book. Thank you for your genuine support. It means the world to have such a beautiful network of people that want to see me succeed. I love every one of you.

Tony and Patty Morrone, Jennifer Ernst, Billy Rottkamp, and Claudia Arnold. Thank you for always hyping up *Struck Inside Out* and helping me believe in my own success. Your support means everything to me.

My Johnny Russell and EGP patrons. Thank you for being

curious about my dreams and asking about my book week after week. A special thanks to Scott Russell, Daniel Ward, Marc Peletier, Billy Wallace, William Bennett, Donnie McCarthy, Christopher Powers, and Erik Heintz who have been requesting this book since 2019.

My students at HECS. Working with you in my creative writing classes and workshopping parts of this book are some of my greatest highlights throughout the last few years. Thank you for being brave enough to share your writing with me. Thank you for inspiring me to be a better teacher. You all have a special place in my heart.

Gabrielle Urena. Thank you for always being my number one fan. You've read all my writing, attended all my workshops, and have been a genuine source of support and encouragement throughout the last few years. You are so special. It has been a privilege to be your "mentor." Thank you for being you.

My Instagram, Facebook, and blogging community. You have made my life rewarding and fulfilling. Every comment. Every message. Every reply to my Sunday Session newsletters. Your support of my journey has made it so much more meaningful. I don't think I can find the words to say how much your readership means to me.

Many thanks to the talented individuals who helped me make *Struck Inside Out*.

My editor, Lia Ottaviano. Your knowledge, creativity, and guidance shaped *Struck Inside Out* into a daily companion that will reach more people. Thank you for teaching me the essential art of killing many darlings.

My book cover designer, Richard Ljoenes. Thank you for creating the cover I always imagined for my first book. Your designs are what dreams are made of.

My typesetter, Phillip Gessert. Thank you for being

patient with me during the early stages of this process. It was a pleasure to work with you.

My proofreader, James Bullivant. You came through for me on such short notice and answered my numerous emails without hesitation. Thank you for helping me with the final touches for this book.

Nicole Adair, who wrote the epigraph to *Struck Inside Out,* and has become a friend through our writing community on Instagram. You are not only an incredible writer but a beautiful person I feel honored to know.

Craig D'Silva, who took photographs for Struck Inside Out's merch line and captured my author headshot. Thank you for your expertise, kindness, and humor. Let's continue to create content together and laugh at each other throughout the process.

And finally, my gratitude to the past.

My past loves on whom most of *Struck Inside Out* is based. Thank you for showing me how powerful a broken heart can be. Thank you for tearing down walls I had to rebuild on my own. Thank you for teaching me self-trust, love, and reliance. Thank you for leading me to my life's greatest romance so far.

My past selves, the seeds that grew this book. I no longer look at you with regret, shame, or disapproval. You are perfect exactly as you are. Keep blooming. I love you.